HONEY, WHO STOLE THE KIDS?!

Here's to beating
the E-Zone!.
Best,

[signature]

"HONEY, WHO STOLE THE KIDS?!"

How to cure your children + yourself of the need to be constantly entertained

GREGORY BLOOM

Action Publishing Group

Printed in the United States of America.

Published by Action Publishing Group
9249 S. Broadway, Suite 200-140
Highlands Ranch, CO 80129
Cover by Michael Monte Moore and Jacinto Hernandez
Illustrations by Jacinto Hernandez

Second Edition

ISBN 978-1-4276-3349-8

If you would like to purchase bulk quantities of this book please
call 1-888-828-3663 or visit
www.honeywhostolethekids.com

This book is dedicated to my best friend and wife, Christy, and to my four children, Johanna, Nicole, Jonathan and Gretchen. Thank you for working together to recover our family from the entrapments of the 'Entertainment Zone.'

Thank you also to my dear friend and colleague, Nathan Martin, for all your assistance and encouragement.

Contents

Preface

 As a father of four beloved children, my primary motivation for writing this book was my concern over the amount of time my own children were spending with the electronic devices available to them in our home. My kids were especially watching too much TV and too many movies! Our family life was slowly deteriorating and our attitudes and relationships with each other were gradually declining.   Being alarmed, I started doing research in a quest to discover what others were finding out about the effects of today's electronics and entertainment options. I wanted to know if I was accurate in my observations, and more importantly I wanted to know how to fix my family's apparent entertainment addiction problems. After spending time thinking about and researching these issues, I realized that my children were becoming addicted to electronics and entertainment *because I myself had unknowingly become addicted and had led by example.*

 Over the course of researching and writing this book,

I've talked with hundreds of families about the growing concern that the electronics revolution can lead our children down an unhealthy road. Many parents have shared my observations about the negative consequences of the entertainment-saturated culture in which we live, but feel as though there is little remedy or much they can do to undue the damage that has been done. In short, they feel somewhat helpless. Other parents I've talked to see little problem at all with the time their children spend daily with electronic devices. A few have even said to me that to deny their children all the new and innovative technological advances available would be to cheat them out of the fullest childhood possible and may even hinder their future. Some busy parents honestly confess that electronic diversions are the only way they can keep their kids calm and occupied most of the time. But that's admittedly intended as a temporary fix, and is a less than ideal solution.

Whatever their viewpoint, I'm concerned that parents may be unwittingly placing a serious obstacle in front of their children by unreservedly embracing and encouraging the proliferation of electronic devices in our homes. In reality, if we fail to help our kids balance their inputs and influences when they are young, they will quickly reach a point where our influence becomes negligible. Ultimately, our window of opportunity with our kids is very narrow, so we of course want to get it as right as we can, while we can.

With that intent, this book is primarily written to parents, grandparents and caregivers of children. It's a simple, common-sense appeal to begin with a self-evaluation of how electronic diversions and excessive entertainment are affecting your family. It's written to those who see little remedy to fix the damage that's already been done and it's written as well to those who believe there isn't much of a problem. Hopefully, I'll be able to convince you that there really is a balance that needs to be struck, and there really are ways to overcome the challenges we face in this age of constant distractions. It's my sincere desire that this book will be helpful to you and your family, and that you will see there's a better way to raise our children than to watch them be overcome by electronic diversions and entertainment addictions.

A few minutes of personal introspective "quiet time" at the gym before the hectic day begins.

INTRODUCTION

Welcome to the Entertainment Zone!

Ah, life in the twenty-first century! Yes, it's wonderful in so many ways compared to twenty, fifty, or a hundred years ago. There've been hundreds of technological, medical, and quality-of-life breakthroughs, all easing our workloads and expanding our leisure lives. And as for entertainment, we've now found ourselves living in what I'm calling the "Entertainment Zone." Who would want to go back to phones tethered to a wall, 45 RPM records, operator-dialed long-distance, or three fuzzy black-and-white TV channels?

It is now possible for us to be entertained during every waking moment of the day.

One of the technological advances that may *seem* better today is all of the varied entertainment options available to us through television, computers, cell phones, computerized games and music. It's everywhere, at anytime! We can watch our favorite TV shows whenever we want with the convenience of Digital Video Recorders. High Definition Television has finally arrived and we can watch full-color, almost life-sized images in near perfect resolution. We can choose between 150 channels of shows, watch tons of full-length movies, view cartoons in the car, play computer games on a hand-held device, listen to satellite radio, surf the Net, spend hours on video gaming, or listen to our favorite downloadable songs on our portable MP3 Players. We can watch television as we exercise at the gym. We can access computers from work, or from practically anywhere in the world. From wherever we are, our pocket sized devices enable us to watch TV shows and movies, play games, listen to hours of music, send pictures and videos, receive text messages, and soon enough we may be able to "beam up" to the *Enterprise!* The list of entertainment options available to us grows more diverse and more potentially distracting each and every day.

We can easily let an entire day slip away by being captivated with a video game (if you don't believe this, you haven't played any lately.) Check out how many of our children wait in line for a full day (or overnight) at the store just to buy a new release of the latest game or gaming machine. Then there's the constant barrage of advertisements designed to appeal to a kid's desire to have the next, newest, latest and greatest games. Instead of walking and talking with their friends, kids walk to school "plugged in" to hours of unedited music. MP3 players are embedded in sunglasses, underwater headphones, tennis shoes, hats, and may soon be implanted in your head!

Individually and collectively, these electronic diversions feed our growing appetite for entertainment. We're becoming addicts almost unknowingly, and we barely notice our own behavior changing. We're either partially oblivious or we're in willful denial. Yet the signs and symptoms of this detrimental condition are all around us. Even more troubling is that fact that we end up, however inadvertently, raising our own children to be little entertainment addicts as well.

We've found ourselves in the middle of an insidious problem that if not directly addressed could cripple the well-being of our families. If we as individuals don't face this issue now, we're insuring a future that will have us all so electronically dependent that *everything* imaginable will have to be entertaining to keep our attention. Whether we're in school, waiting in line, riding in the car, eating, socializing, trying to fall asleep or trying to wake up, our electronic devices will always need to be on. (This is not a hard prediction to make, since it's almost that way now, and I believe it can only get worse.) We'll have to be entertained 24/7, along every path we take during our routine day. We will never have to endure even a five-minute period of silence. Even if we go camping to "get away from it all," our portable electronics will be our constant companions. Soon, we could all have receivers embedded into our earlobes so when we walk into the local coffee shop, wireless networking will download music and advertisements directly into our brains!

As a result of this modern phenomenon, our generation will be the first to suffer from a host of hurtful consequences. They'll be poorer students, who won't have the attention span to study at their full potential. They'll dislike

3

school altogether, because classes will just be too boring. They will miss out on those meditative periods of silence that give rise to the wonders of childhood imagination. They'll be out of tune with their own consciences. They won't want to do anything unless it's audiovisually "fun." They'll forfeit opportunities to participate in sports, clubs, or part-time jobs, because nothing will be able to compete with their desire to remain electronically stimulated at home. They'll compare themselves to the sexy, popular, and rich idols they desire to emulate, and will devalue themselves. They will be constantly discontent with what they have because all they see is what they *don't have.* A great number of them will be misdiagnosed with Attention Deficit Disorder simply because they're restless, and will end up depending on prescription medications.

Today's kids are fast becoming overweight and are generally unhealthy due to a lack of physical activity in their young lives. Many have no hobbies outside of those they find amply supplied in their own bedrooms. They're less likely to know how to relate with people as individuals and have diminished social skills in general. Kids are becoming so accustomed to indirect interaction with people that they feel awkward in the real world around real people, and sometimes even avoid them. They have such constant access to their electronically connected friends that they are rarely influenced by anyone outside of their peer groups. Why would they feel the need to be heard by their parents when they think the whole world is already listening to them through their computers?

It's become painfully obvious that kids are seeing so many images of violence and nudity, and they're hearing so much nonsense and profanity that their minds are becoming numbed to the point that nothing shocks them anymore. We often hear it said that "kids just grow up so fast these days." But is that really what "growing up" is supposed to be? Every year, media writers are pushing the "shock value" envelope further and further as the networks and movie producers battle for viewers in an increasingly competitive commercial entertainment market. There are less and less protections available to parents who value the preservation of their children's innocence. Television and Movie ratings have become practically useless in predicting what twisted content kids will have flashed in their faces.

Is it any wonder when kids complain about how boring school is? Should we be surprised when our children don't want to go to church unless it's entertaining? (It's no shock to notice that contemporary churches already resemble movie theatres or concert stages.) Why would they want to go anywhere or experience anything that might not match the stimulation level they're assured of by just staying home?

Perhaps you're reading this and thinking that *this is already happening*. You are right- it is already happening at an alarming rate, and it will continually get worse if we don't personally do something different. Continuing to do nothing only assures us of the same inevitable results.

Is *all* entertainment bad?

No, it's certainly not all bad. Just as in other areas of life, balance is the key. This book is about restoring balance in our homes; it is about making smart choices. It's about recognizing that there *is* a problem. I'm calling on parents to be discerning about their entertainment choices, and to know what their children are being exposed to. The health of our children's minds and lives are at stake. *The goal of this book is to have you stop and think about how much time you and your family spend passively plugged into the "Entertainment Zone" (henceforth referred to as the E-Zone.)* Just as we'd never have our children eat all the time, sleep all the time, study all the time, play all the time; we should not allow them to be entertained *all* the time.

Just how much time are we spending in the E-Zone?

Children spend more time watching television than any other activity except sleeping. The television is on over seven hours a day in the average U.S. home.[1] The average American watches over four hours per day of television.[2] Sixty-five percent of American children, ages 8-18 years, have a television in their bedroom.[3] Eighty-nine percent of school-aged kids own video-game equipment.[4]

On average, U.S. children who have video games at home play them ninety minutes per day.[5]

By the time our kids reach the age of retirement, they'll

Prayer Needs

have spent *three years of their lives watching just the commercials.*[6] 58% of families with children have the TV on while they eat dinner.[7]

I'll offer more statistics later, but the point I want to make right now is this: *We've been letting the E-Zone raise our children.* And because *it* is raising our children, our children are being raised with the values promoted by commercial interests instead of our personal values.

Every human being orders his or her life based on a set of values and a certain perspective regarding what the world is like. All children wonder who they are, what the world out there is like, and how they fit in. Our children are arriving at a world view based on the influences they're exposed to during their formative years. A child wants to know what's normal and inwardly asks, "Am I normal?" To find out what "normal" is, the child first looks to their family, and then out into the world to define normalcy (e.g., how to dress, how to talk, what to eat, what to believe, and other choices.) Our children form their world-view by the experiences and influences they have while growing up. Sadly, the E-Zone is influencing our children more than we as parents are, because our children spend more time there than they spend with us.

As parents, we ourselves have become addicted to the E-Zone. If we're not being entertained, we too are bored. Even more dangerous than the addiction is the denial that it exists. Many people don't recognize it as a problem and don't think there's anything wrong with being over-entertained; it's just part of life in the twenty-first century— like automobiles, airplanes, and microwave ovens.

But there *is* a problem. We *are* addicted and we must recognize it. In Chapter Two, we'll look into the lives of several families and how their lives revolved around the E-Zone. At the end of the book, I'll provide a Recovery Plan for overcoming insidious E-Zone influences. If overcoming this addiction is not something you'll consider for yourself, please at least remain open-minded for the benefit of your children and your grandchildren. Their core thinking develops from infants to young adults in just a few short years.

A child's development is often described as a combination of nature and nurture— it's the nurture part of the equation that we should be concerned about, because the E-Zone has taken over too much of the nurturing. Nurturing for we parents means coaching, teaching, influencing and caring for our children. Nurturing takes time and it takes commitment. Children need solid foundational roots laid down before the intense challenges of young adult life confront them. As a society and as parents we've not adequately protected our children's development from the rapid advances of the media age. We've allowed the E-Zone to creep into our homes by impulsively purchasing all the newest techno-gadgets and by warmly welcoming unfiltered media to stream into our living spaces.

The debate over media influence on our society has largely been confined to ineffectual academic studies and token senate hearings. It has not yet come to the forefront of national mainstream consciousness in an adequate way. This must change. This is not a problem that will be solved by the academics or the political elite in our society. It certainly won't be solved by the media giants themselves. This is *our* problem to solve.

ONE

How We Become Addicted to the E-Zone

When my older sister, my younger brother and I were growing up, we could watch at most a few hours a day of television. TV shows were simpler and there were far fewer of them to choose from. We didn't have VCRs or DVDs, cable or satellite. All we had was a TV with an antenna on the roof of the house. I remember watching reruns of "I Love Lucy," "The Beverly Hillbillies," and "Gilligan's Island," almost every day after school. We would turn on the TV as soon as we got home to get in our typical one to two hours of viewing. When Dad or Mom got home from work, it was all over; the TV was either turned off or Dad tuned into the evening news for 30 minutes or an hour. There was no such thing as 24/7 news programs.

As the years went by, our one-to-two-hour-a-day TV habit progressed as the television programming progressed. My father, brother, and I became addicted to that weekly football game we couldn't miss. My parents purchased a device called a VCR in the early '80s, and with this new invention, we now had *way* more viewing opportunities each week! Mom and Dad joined the newly opened video rental store in town and we all started watching two to three movies a week! While I was a teenager in the 1980s, cable television started becoming very popular. Cable wasn't available on the farm I lived on, but many of my city friends had it, so I spent a lot of Friday nights at my buddy Darrel's house because he had HBO and MTV! As for video games, we had a local arcade where we played Pinball, Pac Man, and Asteroids. None of us had computers or video games in our homes, so all the games we played were at the local arcade or bowling alley. We had just begun to see computers in our schools, but they were very primitive. I eventually bought a Texas Instruments computer that hooked into our TV at home and I learned how to program it in Basic.

Does this sound similar to your own story? Think about your experiences growing up; each of us has our own unique electronics history, based on when and where we grew up. The progression of new technologies and entertainment options we've laid hold of has been obvious. But noticing how sneakily their influence has laid hold of us is not always so obvious…

The E-Zone revolution boom

My generation experienced small advances in the entertainment revolution, but it's nothing like the generation after us has experienced. Recent advances in technology and entertainment have been truly amazing. Today's children are growing up in an environment that can only be described as "entertainment-super-saturation-land." Let's consider some developments in electronics and the entertainment revolution that we have recently experienced: Cable and Satellite TV with an ever-growing list of channels to choose from, multi-format DVD players, faster and faster computers and computer connections, (DSL, Broadband, WiFi, etc.) the exponentially expanding Internet, websites that allow users to instantly upload pictures and videos for all the world to see, social networking websites, hosts of amazing software advances, HDTV, flat-screen technology, TIVO and DVR's, home-entertainment systems, downloadable songs, downloadable TV shows, downloadable movies, MP3 players, cell phones with cameras and video-viewing capabilities, extreme graphics video-game devices, and TVs in cars, airplanes, stores, banks, gyms, etc. I'm constantly amazed to see a TV in some new place that makes no sense whatsoever, like in an elevator or in a bathroom or on a refrigerator door, to mention just a few.

In what direction is this boom in technology blowing us? Corporate profiteers are insuring us a mass of constantly emerging technologies: like mini-discs the size of a dime that will replace the DVD, MP3 players so tiny that you'll hardly notice them at all, and giant flat screens that take up an entire wall. Almost every car will soon come with standard view screens, satellite links and GPS. With 3-D TV in the development stages, in a few years kids will be asking, "What - you watched TV in just 2 dimensions? How boring!"

Soon, the portable devices we all carry around will

become a singular hybrid; a "personal info-tainment device" that will blow away anything we've seen to date. It will connect us to everyone in our world with a dizzying array of communication options. It will direct voice commands through our phone to be instantly converted into text that's inserted into our appointment calendars and "to-do" lists on our home computers. It will be continuously linked to the all-knowing internet, so that we can have answers to any question the moment we ponder it. It will allow us to interface with our computerized home-controllers so we can order a special section of our fridge to turn itself into an oven and begin cooking a pre-prepped dinner. It will hold sufficient memory to store our daily video diaries and home movies. It will enable us to download any programming we desire on-demand, so we can watch or listen to whatever we want, or play whatever video games we want. It will almost make the people we used to depend upon for help and companionship obsolete.

Not only will our portable devices become incrementally more powerful, what we now call a home desktop computer will also be radically transformed. Devices are now being developed that take the shape of a flat horizontal surface the size of a table. They will be able to instantly interact with any portable device laid on top of them, and their user interface will be similar to the touch screens and smart boards already in use; only as if they were on steroids. Voice recognition and rapid finger-dragging will become more common than the old fashioned keyboard and mouse. User preferences will be automatically detected through usage habits.

Monitoring the user's reaction times and vital signs will enable the computer to adjust its suggestions to maximize its own usefulness.

This all seems exciting, doesn't it? Whenever a new device comes out that enhances our chances of being entertained, we consider it an advancement. We think we've got to keep up with the times and have every new technology (our kids definitely think this and help convince us.) The old devices are no longer good enough because the new ones are thinner, smaller, cooler, and do more "stuff." The savvy marketers that deliver the E-Zone to us know how to market their goods to our kids, because if the kids want it, they'll get it somehow. But is this really progress? As soon as those "new" devices saturate the marketplace, the next generation of upgrades and innovations will be stocked on store shelves to take their place. Will we have to sign up for continuous courses to learn how to use all of these next, newest gadgets? Technophiles may salivate for the latest releases of these sparkling super-toys, but should we all stand in line behind them to sign up for this endless succession of time-suckers disguised as time-savers? We may have cooler gadgets, but how will we maintain healthy relationships if we're so readily distracted? Should we allow the E-Zone to displace time spent with real people? Do we really want the E-Zone deflecting our affections from the people we love?

Why we've become addicted to the E-Zone

The power of the E-Zone lies in its ability to capture our minds with its combination of brilliant audio and video images. It wasn't always this way. The radio programs of the 40's and 50's were not reality substitutes to us. They were endearing stories that led our minds to dream of far away places and encouraged our imaginations, much like reading a book would. Early television showed us innocuous visual images, like the Lone Ranger riding away from the bandits shouting, "Hi-Oh Silver." It was entertaining, but the images were not realistically compelling enough to cause us to believe that we could be him, or that we could do the things he was doing. It was not a simulated reality, but more like a fairy-tale story to our minds, and we recognized it as such.

When it comes to modern entertainment, however, high production values, realistic special effects, and high quality audio-visual equipment completely overwhelm our senses and quickly bind our minds to the stories told by contemporary screenwriters. This gives them a powerful advantage. Can you imagine what it would be like if today's TV writers were constrained to the written page, so that all writers competed on a level playing field? How well do you think the TV writers stories would sell if they were robbed of their multicolored media delivery system? If people couldn't see the shows, but had to read the scripts that shows are based on, their appetite for stupid sitcoms and implausible dramas would dry up in a heartbeat. Take away the fantasy-hungry public's option of having all of these stories beamed

16

into their passive brains through their eyeballs, and they might be more inclined to exercise their minds through the process of reading and imagining higher quality materials. But sadly, the practice of reading is lost to many people, and the quality of the material they take in is controlled by network programmers instead of their own curiosities and interests. People accept the cheaper stories primarily because they are spoon-fed to them through the electrically powered sights and sounds that have replaced imagination.

Half of a human's concentration is said to be devoted directly or indirectly to visual input. Our eyes are undoubtedly the primary input to our brains and, along with the ears, provide the two doors to our minds that allow us to process the sounds and images we experience. When you sit your child down in front of a TV, a movie, or a computer game, you are in essence plugging their brain into that medium, and that medium will fully engage the child's mind until it is turned off.

Our addiction to the E-Zone is based in this reality. We are by nature audiovisual creatures, and the E-Zone fascinates, grips, and overwhelms our audiovisually stimulated minds so that we cannot easily leave it. Even when we do pull away, we still crave the sensations it gives us so much that we go right back to it at the earliest opportunity. An addiction has been defined as, "a complex, progressive, injurious, and often disabling attachment to a substance or activity in which a person compulsively seeks a change of mood."[8] The E-Zone definitely affects our mood. We go to it to relax and unwind, to escape from our day or our circumstances, or to stimulate our senses and pick us up. You probably know many people who say they watch TV or surf the Net as a way to relax, unwind, or escape from reality. Young people will tell you that the E-Zone helps them to "cope" with life. Many will even admit that they "couldn't live without it."

But the E-Zone can be a deceptive trap, because we can't ultimately find what we truly need in it. Many go to the E-Zone to find purpose (like the teens who have to conquer a video game for peer acceptance) or fulfillment (like the temporary but fleeting feeling you have after watching dramatically powerful or motivating movies.) But the E-Zone can't possibly give us the lasting, impacting, meaningful relationships with other people and with our Creator that we desperately need to grow, develop, and prosper as human beings. Our E-Zone addiction draws from us and empties us instead of filling us. We have to admit this to ourselves if we are honest. We've been there and done that, so to speak. We just sit down to watch the evening news to unwind, but after being sucked into a few hours of it, we are left tired, empty, discouraged, and drained of all our energy and emotion (due in part to the fact that our consciences have been numbed by the constant barrage of violent images, bad news and discouragement we just subjected ourselves to.) I have a friend who radically refers to a TV as "a device that sucks our souls out through our pupils." While that may be an overstatement, at the very least, the E-Zone does a powerful job of captivating us, while leaving us wanting more. Like a thirst that's never quenched, we keep drinking from the E-Zone well because it tastes so good at the moment. We're trading time that could be used to build something lasting for something that's definitely momentary. We are like the proverbial frogs in the boiling pot, not noticing that what's making us comfortable is slowly stealing our lives. We continue craving it even though we know it's not good for us. How can this not be defined as an addiction?

TWO

The Results of E-Zone Parenting

"The television is an invention that permits you to be entertained in your living room by people you wouldn't have in your home." —David Frost

In this chapter, let's briefly examine the E-Zone experiences of three different families: one family with young children, one family with a single mom raising three kids, and one family with teenagers. We'll see that the E-Zone turns children into addicts while they are quite young, and captivates them throughout their formative years and beyond. I'll conclude the chapter with the story of a very good friend of mine who works at a state university. He will help us discover that by the time our children get to college the damage has been done and it is very difficult to remedy the destructive effects of long term E-Zone addiction. The following stories are all true, with only the names changed so as not to embarrass family members.

A Family Raising Young Children

Joe and Tammy have three small children aged two, four and seven. They never viewed any of the recent advances in entertainment as good or bad; they just accepted them as part of the new world in which we all live. But they realized that their three children were not benefiting from all this "cool" technology. In fact, they discovered that their marriage, their family, their personal and spiritual growth, and their children's development were all suffering. They had all slowly and unknowingly become addicted to entertainment and the technology that provided it. They had adopted these new media technologies into their homes and made them virtual family members. Joe and Tammy had VHS, DVD, Netflix, a membership at several local video rental stores, a video game box, cable, DSL, a new fast computer with speakers and games, cell phones . . . and almost all of their discretionary time was spent with them.

When the kids got up they watched TV before school. When they all got home from school or work, they wanted to watch TV or surf the 'Net or play games. After the kids were put to bed, Tammy and Joe would watch one of those weekly TV drama shows that they'd gotten addicted to viewing religiously. Most of the time Joe wasn't sleeping through the night, so he'd watch the 24-hour news channels when he couldn't sleep. If the news started getting too repetitive, Joe would start flipping through the 150 channel choices on the remote. For Joe's birthday, Tammy bought him a computer game and he became obsessed with it. Joe could spend the entire evening, or several hours in the middle of the night, climbing levels. It took him about a month and a half of constant playing, for hours at a time, until he was finally a champion! He had completed all the levels and beaten up all the bad guys. Joe thought he'd had enough and that he needed a break from forty-five days of playing, but just then they released the sequel. Joe got it for Father's Day!

Joe was getting up each day only half-rested and was irritable much of the time. He used coffee and caffeinated drinks to stay awake during the day. Joe could stay awake as long as he was moving around, but if he had to sit for anything over thirty minutes, he'd have to fight against dozing. Joe had a headache most of the time—not a severe one, just an annoying, constant, dull ache behind his eyes. Tammy, who was less addicted to the E-Zone than Joe was, became very concerned about the amount of time Joe was spending in the E-Zone. Joe considered "quality time" with Tammy and the kids to be watching a movie or a football game together. Joe *had* to watch his college alma mater play football on the weekends, then the pro football games on Sunday. By Sunday night, when the weekend was over, he might have spent six to ten total hours, or more, in front of sports TV and less than an hour, or no time at all, one-on-one with his children. Meanwhile, Joe and Tammy weren't happy with their children's attitudes and behavior . . . but *they* had been subjecting them to further addiction to the E-Zone via their own addiction.

A Single Parent Family

Terri is a single-mom raising her three children aged nine, eleven and fourteen. Her ex-husband lives two hours away and has the kids with him every other weekend. Terri works a 9 to 5 job, but she very often gets home after 6 p.m. Her oldest son Jeff takes care of his siblings until Mom gets home. Jeff gets home from middle-school everyday at 2:45 p.m. He is supposed to do his homework as soon as he gets home, but he gets distracted by the internet and his video game library most days and can't seem to get to his homework. Jeff's little sister and brother get home from elementary school an hour after Jeff arrives. They immediately turn on the TV, grab some snacks and watch the Disney Channel until Mom gets home. Terri doesn't like the fact that her kids are spending so much time in the E-Zone, but she would rather keep the kids in her own house than have them out in the streets or over at an unknown friend's house. Terri's two younger children have electronic pocket pets. They got them from Grandma as birthday gifts. The kids are fascinated with them and can't leave their E-Zone pets alone for more for than 30 minutes at a time. Terri tolerates the electronic pocket pets at the dinner table, in the car, by the bedside and everywhere the kids go during the day, but she is troubled by the children's fascination with caring for their virtual pets.

Terri's kids spend 4 to 8 hours a day in the E-Zone, but Terri feels she can't do anything about it. Terri is dead tired when she gets home from work, and usually brings some work home with her. With the limited amount of time that she does have to spend with her children, she tries to help with their homework. Almost every night the family eats dinner in front of the TV. Dad comes by every other week to pick up the kids and usually takes them out to dinner and a movie. When the kids return Sunday evening from Dad's house, Terri discovers that the kids spend a good portion of Saturday and Sunday watching sports on TV with dad or playing video games.

A Family Raising Teenagers

Todd and Sue have two teen-aged boys, ages fourteen and seventeen. Several years ago Sue bought iPods for her two boys for Christmas. They were expensive, but it was what the boys wanted. Todd and Sue figured that the boys would listen to the iPods about as much as they listened to their older portable CD players—just once in a while. The parents were quite alarmed when the boys went everywhere with the iPods. Todd and Sue thought that it would last for just a couple of weeks, until the newness of the gifts wore off, then things would get back to normal. They were wrong. The boys spend much more time with their iPods than they did with the old portable CD players. With the CD players, the boys would get a new album occasionally, but with the iPods, they can download new songs daily. The boys have developed an unhealthy attachment to the devices, and they take them everywhere they go. Todd and Sue used to have some quality time with their sons in the car as they drove around town, but not anymore, because the boys are always "plugged in." Also Todd and Sue used to be able to listen to what the boys were listening to and they could monitor the songs and lyrics of the music tunes. With the iPods, Todd and Sue really don't know on a daily basis what the boys are hearing. All of this bothers Todd and Sue. They tried to encourage the boys to give away the iPods, but they won't think of it. So to deal with their sons' addiction to their iPods, Todd and Sue are forced to take iPod privileges away from the boys as a form of discipline (i.e., when the boys do not finish their chores or homework, they lose iPod privileges that day).

Todd and Sue's boys also have cell phones. The parents wanted their sons to have a way to reach them when they were apart. It especially gave mom a lot of comfort knowing that she could reach them or they could call her when needed. The phones provide a good channel of communication for family members, but have some unwanted side effects. The boys use the phones to text message, play games, watch TV and talk to their friends. Todd and Sue had to disconnect the video and text messaging components of the phones because their sons can easily spend hours each day sending and receiving messages from their friends at school. Todd and Sue are tired of having to constantly monitor the amount of time their sons are spending in the E-Zone. Sue says that she is always the "bad mom" that has to limit or lecture the boys on not spending all their time in the E-Zone. They always come back with the expected retort: "But our friends get to," whenever she has to take away the phones, iPods, video games or DVDs. Todd and Sue told me that they wish they had never gotten these devices in the first place, but that now it's impossible to get rid of them.

Young Adults Raised by E-Zone Parenting

Do you ever wonder what kind of young adult E-Zone parenting produces? I have a friend who supervises college workers on a university campus in New England. He has great difficulty hiring students who possess even a remnant of what used to be called a work ethic. These "young adults"—who should have long ago learned a considerable degree of adult responsibility—can't be left alone unsupervised. They are constantly leaving their work unfinished and running back to their computer stations. It seems to be the only place they feel comfortable. As long as their cell phone is in texting mode, and as long as their high speed, networked computer is simultaneously displaying their multiple instant messaging conversations, email-alerts, live-competition video gaming window, multimedia music player, and their most recently downloaded movie, they are momentarily happy. He describes them as "electronic black-holes," insatiably consuming any and all E-Zone stimulation available to them. They are not at all satisfied with becoming E-Zone multi-taskers; they aspire to become E-Zone *poly-taskers*—doing all things electronic at all times.

When the time comes to rouse these E-Zone "poly-taskers" from their perpetually over-stimulated mental state to actually do some work, their initial response is that dazed glare that, without words asks: *"You want me to do what?"*

Who needs the chemical stimulation so popular in the 60's when you've got a dual-core processor to keep you from reality? It sometimes takes several audible requests to evoke an actual verbal response from these "electronically-altered chowder-heads," as my friend from the North East calls them. They're as apathetic as any pot-smoker you've ever met. They actually resent being asked to do work, even when they're being paid. When asked to get to work, they reluctantly struggle to extract themselves from their electronic diversions. Their ambitions seem to extend only to maintaining their E-zone comforts. Absence from their devices leaves them with an instant case of E-Zone separation anxiety. Even brief periods of solitude or quiet are considered to be intolerable isolation to them. Sleep deprivation and minimal attention spans are par for the course.

Now that we have these long-term E-Zone addicts, all we need is for the conscientious hardware and software companies to place warning labels on the sides of all electronic devices and programs. My friend suggests:

> *"Warning: the Surgeon General has determined that excessive electronic stimulation can produce symptoms resembling catatonic states, vegetative comas and/or chemical lobotomies. No government agency has yet developed an effective 12-step program to counteract the highly addictive properties of this device. Results of taxpayer funded studies on the long-term effects of over-usage are now being compiled in the laboratory of your homes and schools. By using*

this product, you automatically agree to participate in these studies as our volunteer. The real-time collection of user data via your DVRs (Digital Video Recorders) will be funded by a variety of corporate sponsors at no cost to you. By order of the Attorney General, the US government cannot be held liable for the contents or consequences of the commercial media dispensed through this device."

I'm afraid even a label this radical would fare no better at curbing E-Zone addictions than the warnings imposed on tobacco products have curbed nicotine addiction for tobacco users. Severe E-Zone addiction at the college level is nearly pandemic today.

He notes that today's college student-workers are quick to stop working every time their cell phone vibrates a nerve in their leg. Voicemail systems require far more patience than these undisciplined kids are willing to expend. Every incoming call is urgent. Every random thought must immediately be shared with anyone who might care to listen. My friend wonders and laments, "How will these people ever become productive human beings?" He tells me there is also a generalized atmosphere of personal isolationism in many educational institutions today. Walking down the hallways of a contemporary college will leave you feeling like you've just visited a home for the deaf. Try asking someone for the time, and he'll turn and ignore you; then you'll notice the tiny earphones lodged in his ears, his music effectively blocking contact with people around him. Don't be too quick to respond to someone talking to you, either, lest he turn his head away and expose the ear phone he's using to carry on the real conversation he's having with someone else.

Technology has also had its effects in approaches to classroom instruction. With the installation of DVD players, high-speed internet, projectors and Smart Boards in most modern classrooms, professors have found that it's easier to electronically teach than prepare actual lectures. The popularization of slide show and PowerPoint presentations has led many educators to substitute the reading of outlines projected on a screen for actual teaching. While software is indeed a useful tool designed to augment the teaching experience, too many times the teacher entirely relies on it as a substitute. Many students are insulted and bored when an un-motivating professor reads their outlines off the wall like a grocery list class after class. Whatever happened to the teacher who engages the hearts, minds and personalities of their students in the attempt to convey truth that meant something to them personally? That's something that many modern students have never had the privilege of experiencing.

One thing is for certain, the corporate 'merchants of cool' can sell pre-packaged rebellion to our teens and young adults in brilliant multimedia fashion more adeptly than the manufacturers of corn syrup can fatten them. As long as college students continue consuming the same mainstream media, they will always share the exact same thoughts and consequent behaviors. Our young adults are being technologically homogenized into a mass of culturally cloned non-thinkers.

It's long been obvious that the efforts of young people to be culturally different from (and thereby somehow superior to) their parents usually ends up with them all being almost exactly alike in their independently adapted 'distinctions.' But we must now recognize that the long term effects of the incremental assimilation of technology and the electronic homogenization of thought are not just cultural. Kids don't just wear different clothes and listen to different music than their parents. The information age, as we are so fond of calling it, has placed remarkably powerful tools into the hands of technologically adept and morally bankrupt children. They possess ready access to an unimaginable mass of data, both good and evil. That makes it easy for young people to become convinced that they possess more intelligence than their predecessors. Ironically, their own intellectual potential is being drained away by the very technology in which they so readily place their confidence.

These observations and comments may seem dramatic, but they are reflective of an increasing pattern in higher education. This is a direct result of E-Zone parenting in America. Ask yourself if you want your child to become what has become of a typical E-Zone raised college kid. Ask yourself how you can help your children rise above the influences and temptations of our time to have a future that is not shaped by the E-Zone.

**"Quality family time" at the Jones'
during the holidays**

THREE

The Replacement of Relationships

"Television has proved that people will look at anything rather than each other."—Ann Landers

"I see my husband and kids everyday, but I rarely talk to them about any of the intimate details of our lives. We talk about movies, TV shows, school and work, but it's all very superficial. No, I can't say that I really know my kids or that they really know me well at all, there is no time to get to know each other anymore." —Mom in Los Angeles, California

Did you spend more time today with the E-Zone than you did your own children? Did your children spend more time in the E-Zone than they did will all family members combined? The most detrimental aspect of Entertainment Addiction is the loss of relationships. Simply put, we don't know one another like we used to. If we don't know each other, then we don't understand each other, because we can no longer connect or relate to one another. If we cannot relate to our children, and our children cannot relate to one another, then we don't function as a family. In a dysfunctional family we don't communicate, and we have very shallow, fragile relationships with our family members. As parents, we cannot speak into our children's lives because there just isn't enough time left over each day. Our children have learned to prefer input from the E-zone over input from parents regarding life issues. At holiday and other family gatherings everyone just wants to sit around and watch television instead of catching up and relating with one another.

The E-Zone has displaced and diminished the family

The Jones family gets together for Thanksgiving each year. It's the only time all the children and grandchildren make it in unison to Dad and Mom Jones' house in up-state New York. You'd think that after a year apart, they'd make an effort to spend some one-on-one quality time with each other, just catching up. You would expect they'd ask each other a sincere "How have you been?" and then await a good, long, intimate answer, instead of just a "Fine, great. And you?" response.

But tragically, the family members' entertainment addiction supersedes the need for family relations. Shortly after arriving at the so-called family reunion, the men (and a few ladies) pile in the front room that has the football game on, the kids all go upstairs to play video games in a spare bedroom, and two or three women help Mom Jones prepare the big meal in the kitchen. Everyone is forced to take a break from their addiction to eat (except for Uncle Mike, who will not miss any of the game, so he gets a plate of food at a commercial break and retreats back to the game room.) At dinner, no one wants to talk a lot for two reasons; 1) their mouths are full of the food they're eating as fast as possible so they can get back to the video and football games, and 2) no one really knows or wants to know about Aunt Janie's cancer, cousin Pete's softball, Uncle Jerry's train collection, Susan's problems with her marriage, Joey's issue at school with grades and girls, or Melinda's new job in the Big Apple. It would take some time to learn about these issues, joys, and concerns. But everyone's subconscious calendar is already booked for more after-dinner entertainment. So dinner is a quiet affair of small talk about the weather, Dad's new wood floors in the dining room, how nice the new, big-screen HDTV is and wow, those new video games are really fun! After only about thirty minutes, dinner together is completed, Mom Jones is praised for another knock-out meal and the family disperses again to the respective Entertainment Zones around the house.

Dad Jones puts in a DVD for the kids in the home-entertainment theatre in the basement (to keep them quiet and from interrupting the football game). The men finish football game one, and go on to the second game. Mom Jones gets her daughter Susan in a corner and forces her to open up about the issues in her life, but it turns into an argument since Susan feels that Mom is just prying and is not genuinely concerned. So Mom Jones goes to the living room, turns on a "ladies" movie for the women to watch together. After a total of six hours of spending this "quality" family time together, when the football game and the movie are over, everyone suddenly becomes very uncomfortable with each other and packs up to leave. As they say their goodbyes, they all politely agree that it has been a wonderful day together and they can't wait until the next time they'll all be together.

Before the Entertainment Zone's influence grew into what it is today, families got together much more frequently and they related to one another much more often. The girls and boys went outside for an impromptu game, or would play using their imaginations. The men would sit on the porch, or in the back yard, and tell stories about fishing trips, or wars, or would work on the car together. The ladies would talk about their life experiences and would gain insights from one another. Telling humorous life stories to each other would help us to relieve our stress and would allow us to view our difficult circumstances with a better perspective. Rather than going to the TV to find superficial laughter, we enjoyed genuine belly-laughs sharing our joys and troubles with each other. Our brothers and sisters are the only ones who can make fun of our past mistakes and tragedies and cause us to laugh at ourselves. Family relationships were deeper, stronger, and much more intimate. We knew each other better and therefore *liked* each other more than we do now. We were comfortable just being together and we weren't bored by spending a day just hanging out with our family group for a day.

Today many parents of teens acknowledge that their children spend the majority of their discretionary time alone in their bedrooms. The children's rooms resemble the NASA control center with the TV screen, DVD player, computer monitor, cell phone, Xbox game player and other E-Zone devices. With all this cool stuff in their rooms, it is no wonder that children prefer to be in their own private E-Zone suite over the dinner table or the family room. The "family room" of old does not actually exist in many homes these days—it has been literally displaced by the E-Zone room.

The E-Zone has affected our relationships with our spouses, our parents, our friends, our co-workers, our bosses, our neighbors, and our Creator. It has even messed up our relationship with ourselves. We don't know who we are or why we are even here (is it to watch six hours of TV a day, play video games, and surf the 'Net?) The E-Zone has definitely isolated us from one another. We can't sit still for two hours anymore and just talk on the back porch; we get bored and uncomfortable with each other. We now relate with each other through the phone, text messages, the Internet, video conferences, and an assortment of electronic video screens. We now live our lives in the E-Zone from birth to death. Our nation's toddlers meet the E-Zone after just a few days on Earth and become addicted to it before they can walk or talk.

FOUR

An Example of a Typical E-Zone Addicted Family

"I think that parents only get so offended by television because they rely on it as a babysitter and the sole educator of their kids."— Trey Park and Matt Stone, authors of the controversial animated TV program *South Park*

"The kids are happier watching TV than they are talking to me anyway, plus I can get a lot more work done if they are not in my way." — Work-at-home dad in Denver, CO.

Karen and Ben have three children who are E-Zone addicts. It all started many years ago, when without a thought, Karen sat one child down at a time after they were born (Johnny, Ashlee, and Karlie) in front of the TV each day. The TV-Nanny took care of the kids so that Mom could get some work done around the house. One hour quickly turned into two hours. After a while, two hours turned into three hours, as Mom left the kids under the supervision of the TV-Nanny so she could work from home in her bustling real estate career. At the same time, Ben's leadership and influence had been largely replaced. Ben worked late and was too tired when he did come home to relate to anyone, so the DVD player spent two hours each day telling stories to and spending time with the kids after dinner. The kids amassed an impressive video library of over 200 titles, some of which had been viewed over a dozen times. However, as they got older, the animated "kid shows" weren't working like they once did. So Ben and Karen paid for another Nanny in the form of a video game box and a few games. The game console was waiting there every day with an adventure to stimulate little Johnny. Video Game-Nanny wasn't all bad; she tested the kid's hand-eye coordination and stimulated their reflexes; she showed them gaming strategies and how to play poker. The kids loved her. With so much of their time consumed with TV, DVDs, and Video-Games, the three kids still normally had at least an hour a day to spend on the internet. The internet took the kids all over the world and showed them sensational sights, including some they shouldn't see. It was a quick help with homework and could recall amazing facts about any subject in just a few seconds. The internet became a reliable, yet irresponsible Babysitter. But at least the kids got along with her.

Karen asked her husband Ben (they both sincerely want nothing but the best for their three kids) to put in a bigger HDTV and a surround-sound system. Ben was glad to oblige—and it would also be a good setup for football! Ashlee and Karlie watched two movies every day in their new ultimate home-theater. For birthdays, the kids all got new movies or video games. Johnny mastered at least twenty games, and plays other kids all over the world via the internet.

He has conquered all the levels and has a website where he blogs every day about tips and tricks he has discovered to get to the next levels. Johnny has become so good with the games he plays, he just won a local contest and was awarded $1000 in prize money. His dream is to make a living like a virtual athlete by playing and winning video games all over the world.

As the kids grew up, dinner table discussions centered more and more on conversations about their favorite electronic appetites. After a while, Karen and Ben decided they couldn't even compete at the table with the E-Zone anymore. They gave in and put the TV on during dinner. Now the electronics are practically always on, spending in excess of seven hours a day with Johnny, Ashlee, and Karlie. The TV greets them the moment they get home from school each day. Video Games are right behind, spending more time each week with the kids as they get older. The new Internet-Babysitter now spends the most time with Johnny, as he is a teenager, but she's spending more time with the younger girls now that they have their own computer.

This has sadly become a typical family story. Average American children are watching in excess of four hours of TV every single day. That's more time than they spend with their fathers or mothers in quality one-on-one time *all week*. Our children are easily captivated by the endless stream of bright and flashy stories that are dramatically acted out in two-dimensional fantasies. Let's face it, the E-Zone is very exciting. It offers something for everyone. It is hardly ever boring, and if one electronic component gets boring, another presents a new strategy to keep minds occupied. Electronic influences on the growth, development and behavior of our children is truly staggering. As our children are maturing, their opportunities to develop unique imaginations and goals are co-opted by a virtual tidal wave of distractions. The disappearance of independent thought in kids has led many to seek 15 megabytes of fame on the internet rather than making positive contributions in the real world. They have attained more instant entertainment gratification than the richest Kings of old ever dreamed of, and it has stripped them of all patience. They expect everything to come to them quickly and easily. Our generation had to learn the benefits of working, saving, and waiting for what we wanted. Ironically, in our desire to "make it easier" for our kids, we've robbed them of the very difficulties that taught us some of our most valuable lessons. Electronics do make it easier to learn, to communicate, to navigate, to recreate; and even to cheat, steal, and learn about sex. But is easier automatically better? The E-Zone teaches our children values that are just the opposite of the values that we are trying to teach them (e.g. what is important in life, how to function as a healthy family, how we should treat others, etc.) It's no wonder that new labels like "adultalescents" are now being coined in an effort to describe the emotionally underdeveloped generation that's poised to take the reins of our society.

One great motivator for beating these E-Zone addictions is to think about what will happen to your children if you don't help them now. If E-Zone influences are replacing Mom and Dad's, then the people your children grow up to be will more closely resemble the poor role models they watch on TV than you! Your children are spending more precious time each day with MTV, stupefying sit-coms, and "un-reality TV" than they are with you, and those personalities will no doubt influence them more than you. Even in the more rare cases when the programming is good, we can end up trading what's just plain "good" for time that could be much better spent.

Do your kids talk back to you, and refuse to listen? Are they disrespectful, lazy, can't seem to sit still or pay attention, seem unmotivated, and are discontent or depressed most of the time? When you do spend time with them, do they act uninterested in the things you want to do or discuss? When you talk to your children, do they complain that you're "riding them," or criticizing their choices and that you don't understand or support them? This is what modern media has taught them. For one thing, self-serving television writers have effected your children far more than you realize, because they have a more influential platform and have spent more time with them than you have. They know exactly how to stimulate your children, how to captivate them, and how to provoke their behavior—with the ideas, values, and perceptions they promote. If you think this is overstated, just notice how the world seems to stop and the withdrawal begins when TV writers go on strike. These masters of the perpetual cliffhanger are obviously working feverishly to keep our curiosity hooked into what's going to happen next. They know how to manipulate and capitalize on our endless curiosities by writing each episode as a giant teaser for the next.

Their expertise assures them that we just can't stand to feel like we've missed something, and they know we have to know what's coming. Night-time dramas are just glorified soap operas that never deliver full resolution or story completion. They've got us right where they want us, standing in line like starving people holding empty bowls at a soup kitchen, desperately begging for the next little morsel of malnourishing addict-o-tainment. They dole it out in controlled doses like drug dealers.

What if we miss some must-see-TV? Oh, no! I missed an episode of one of my shows last night! Not to worry, you can catch an instant re-run on any of the network website's media players the day after it airs. Watching shows this way is becoming so popular that commercial revenues are way up. Entire series are written exclusively for web viewing. The internet is now doubling as the world's communal Digital Video Recorder so we can always have our shows on-demand, never missing a single fix, courtesy of our favorite advertisers. We can even watch re-runs of yesterday's weather reports in case we didn't get a chance to look out the window!

FIVE

Symptoms of Entertainment Addiction

As with any addiction, entertainment addiction has recognizable symptoms that can help you discover if you or your children have it. The Entertainment Addiction Self-Test at the end of the chapter should be helpful in identifying these symptoms.

I've had a few conversations with parents that have gone something like this: "Shouldn't we leave the proper diagnosis and treatment of this disease to the professionals?"

"Who are the professionals?" I ask.

"Pediatricians and child psychologists, I suppose."

"I have four children and we've been to plenty of appointments with pediatricians. I have yet to be asked by the pediatrician anything about how much entertainment my child is getting at home," I state.

"Perhaps you're going to the wrong pediatricians."

"Do you have kids?" I ask, trying to be a polite as possible.

"Yes. Two." (Or three, or six.)

"Has your pediatrician ever asked you about your

children's TV viewing habits, or how much time they spend playing video games, surfing the Internet, or other forms of entertainment?" I ask gently.

"Well, I don't believe my pediatrician would have time for those sorts of questions in the short visits we have with him. He's usually trying to find out what's physically wrong with my child at that particular time."

We cannot expect our children's doctor to know what's going on day-to-day in our homes. We typically only take our children to a medical doctor to get shots or to diagnose a physical problem. Because of the high cost of health care and other factors, we don't take our children to the doctor, nurse, or clinic, for preventive reasons. It's not that these people don't care about our children's entertainment habits; for instance, the American Academy of Pediatrics (AAP) is very much concerned with the affects the Entertainment Zone has on our children. The following abstract summary from the AAP stated:

> The American Academy of Pediatrics recognizes that exposure to mass media (i.e., television, movies, video and computer games, the Internet, music lyrics and videos, newspapers, magazines, books, advertising, etc.) presents both health risks and benefits for children and adolescents. Media education has the potential to reduce the harmful effects of media. By understanding and supporting media education, pediatricians can play an important role in reducing the risk of exposure

to mass media for children and adolescents.[9]

Much of the AAP's resources, available at *aap.org*, are to help *the parents* understand what is most beneficial for the children's health and instructs *parents* on how to make good choices regarding entertainment in the home.

It's not their job; it's yours.

It is not your pediatrician's job to know if your kids are watching too much TV each day; it is your job. It is not anyone else's responsibility but the parents' or other primary caregivers' to ensure that their children are not growing up as entertainment addicts. Despite our "blame-game" society, where we blame everyone else for our problems and our kids' problems, there is no escaping the fact that you are the primary influence in your children's lives. If you are not the primary influence, something is wrong. We cannot blame our children's teachers for our children's low test scores— we should be helping our children with their homework on a daily basis. We cannot blame our church leaders for our children's spiritual apathy—we are the primary teachers of spiritual values to our children by what we tell them and more importantly, how we live with them. We cannot blame our medical or psychological doctors for our child's problems— we only draw upon such professionals after things are already going wrong.

Red flags in our homes

The following survey will help parents recognize some of the symptoms of entertainment addiction. As with other addictions (i.e. to caffeine, tobacco, or alcohol) there are varying degrees of the addiction. One child in a home may have a slight addiction to entertainment, while another may have a serious addiction. One of my children had a serious addiction, while the others had a slight or moderate addiction. Take the test yourself, and then have your children take it. Compare your answers and see if you both agree on the test results. The questions are derived from studies (included later) that reveal the effects of the E-Zone on our children.

Are my children addicted to entertainment?

Score the following statements:
Score: never = 0, sometimes =1, usually =2, almost always=3, always =4

1. My child watches 2 hours or more of TV per day.
2. My child watches TV during meals.
3. My child has a TV, computer, or game machine in his or her bedroom.
4. My child watches TV, plays games, or listens to music before going to school.
5. My child needs the TV or music on to go to sleep at night.
6. My child enjoys watching TV over reading (or having a book read to him.)
7. My child has a hard time sitting still.
8. There are TV shows each week that my child just can't miss.
9. My child hits or pushes other kids often.
10. My child spends most of his non-school hours in the E-Zone.
11. My child has a difficult time sleeping at night.
12. My child has a hard time keeping up with assignments.
13. My child talks back to adults (including parents).
14. My child eats unhealthy foods daily.
15. My child has an iPod or MP3 player and uses it daily.
16. My child struggles with being content with what he has.
17. My child prefers to be entertained over participating in impromptu neighborhood games or activities with other children.

18.   My child complains daily about having to go to school.
19.   My child is struggling with reading.
20.   My child frequently gets into trouble at school with teachers or schoolmates.
21.   My child has a hard time listening.
22.   My child must have the TV or radio on while doing his homework.
23.   My child is overweight.
24.   My child's hero is a famous actor or actress.
25.   My child wants holiday or birthday presents that are E-zone related.
26.   My child spends more than an hour a day playing video games.
27.   My child spends more than 30 minutes each day surfing the net for fun (not homework).
28.   My child prefers to be alone in his room over playing outside with other children.
29.   My child complains a lot that he is bored.
30.   My child watches more than two movies per week.
31.   My child has a cell phone and carries it with him all of the time.

_____ Total Score

Less than 30 points = not likely to have an addiction
31 to 50 points = a slight addiction
51 to 70 points = a moderate addiction
71 to 90 points = a serious addiction
Over 91 points = a critical addiction

SIX

How Bad Is It, Really? What the Research Says

There is nothing more alarming for a parent in our current day than the shootings that are occurring at an ever growing rate in our nation's schools, shopping centers, churches and other public places. If our kids can't be safe at school or the mall or even at church, then where can they be safe? Many parents answer this question by saying, "my kids are safer at home." But are they? It may *seem* like your kids are safer at home because they are physically safe and out of harm's way. However, they are actually in a very dangerous place if while they are home they are left unsupervised in the entertainment zone. As I did the research for this book I was honestly overwhelmed by the findings of the studies that have been released. I could have easily doubled the size of this book by including research that's been done showing the harmful effects that the media and electronic age has inflicted upon the family. The stereotypical family unit (the idea of a family with a mom, dad and kids who spend time together) may be a thing of the past as it has become a casualty of the E-Zone. My intention in writing this book was to make it reasonably readable by keeping it short and to the point, but yet still offer a convincing argument to parents that we are raising our children in a very difficult and precarious time that demands our attention and our action. Addictions to electronic diversions and entertainment are causing real problems in the lives of our children, in our family units, and in society. I believe I have sorted out a good amount of research and offered the "best of the best" here below:

From the moment our kids are born they are being exposed to the E-Zone. A 2007 study found that parents are allowing their babies to watch TV, videos or DVDs so that by three months of age, 40% of infants are regular viewers. By the time the children are two-years-old 90% of them are regular viewers. The parents in the study cited three most common reasons for allowing their young children to view TV, Videos or DVDs. 1) 29% believed these media were educational or good for the child's brain development. 2) 23% said that viewing was enjoyable or relaxing for the child. 3) 21% used these means as babysitter so that parents can do other things at home.[10]

Another study by the University of Washington and the Seattle Children's Hospital research Institute found that the so-called "development" DVDs that parents buy for their toddlers to enhance and stimulate their brain are actually hindering a child's normal mental development.[11]

Parents have a difficult time restricting the amount of time their children spend watching TV because of the following: parents' need to use television as a safe and affordable distraction, parents' own heavy viewing patterns, the significant role that television plays in the day-to-day family routine and the belief that children should be able to use their discretionary leisure time as they so desire.[12]

A New Zealand Study released in 2007 of 1037 participants found that childhood TV viewing was associated with attention problems in adolescence. In this longitudinal study, parental estimates of children's TV viewing time were obtained at ages 5, 7, 9 and 11 years. Self-, parent- and teacher-reported attention problems in adolescence were obtained at 13 and 15 years. These results confirm the hypothesis that childhood TV viewing may contribute to the development of attention problems and that the effects may be long lasting.[13]

In Daxing, China, internet addiction has become such an alarming problem that a military-run installation was built to attempt to cure the patients of their addiction to the internet. The clinic in the suburb of Beijing has 60 patients normally and up to 280 at peak, with patients 12 to 24 years old. Patients are treated with counseling, military discipline, hypnosis, mild electric shock and in severe (and mostly hopeless) cases, drug therapy.[14]

Children in single-parent homes are entertained with media more than children in two-parent homes.[15] This likely reflects the sentiments of many single moms I have talked to, where they prefer the kids to be locked up inside the house over having the kids out in an unknown and uncontrolled environment.

As the amount of TV viewing increases, so do negative outcomes, such as lower school performance,[16] an increased tendency to be overweight[17] (in 2003-2004, 17.1% of U.S. children and adolescents were overweight, and 2.2% were obese,[18] and increased TV viewing time leads to an increase in junk-food intake in adolescents[19]) and a higher likelihood of increased aggression.[20] It is a very difficult time to be a teacher, be it public or private. Students are entertained at home for 4 to 6 hours each day and then sent to school where they have to sit still, behave and concentrate, which many kids are simply untrained to do. Our nation's kids are overweight and getting heavier and are increasing their junk food intake since that is the diet modeled for them (and that their pallets prefer) in the E-Zone. A study released in 2007 by the FTC showed that children are exposed to over 18,000 commercials a year and that over 25% of the commercials are food related. Of those food related commercials, the majority are for foods high in sugar.

Higher amounts of Internet use have been associated with increased loneliness and depression and less communication with others.[21] This study's result should clearly be obvious to us as we see that our children prefer to be isolated in a corner of the house with their "gadget friends" rather than socializing with their friends or siblings. Give a child a choice between a video game or a game of kickball outside and just see what they pick. With decreasing socialization with family members and friends comes isolation and loneliness.

Media content that is high in violence has been linked to fear, desensitization, and a larger appetite for even more violence and increased aggression.[22] This study may have a "ho-hum yawn" response from us because we have become desensitized to the sex, nudity, language and violence progressively portrayed in the media. Our appetite for TV shows, video games, movies and print that portray even more evil violence, more sex, and more provocative drama grows each year.

Higher amounts of video-game playing are correlated with poorer grades.[23] Children who are exposed to greater amounts of video-game violence are more likely to get into physical fights, get into arguments with teachers, and are more hostile.[24] The American Academy of Pediatrics reports that, ". . . more than 1000 studies and reviews have concluded that significant exposure to media violence increases the risk of aggressive behavior in children and adolescents, desensitizes them to violence, and makes them believe that the world is a "meaner and scarier" place than it is."[25]

The average young American viewer is exposed to over 14,000 sexual references each year.[26] In one study, ninth graders were more likely to approve of premarital sex after watching MTV for less than an hour.[27] The number of sexual scenes on television has nearly doubled since 1998 and 70% of all TV shows include some sexual content, and that these shows average five sexual scenes per hour.[28]

The Following is an abstract summary from a 2006 Kaiser Family Foundation report.

Electronic media is a central focus of many very young children's lives, used by parents to help manage busy schedules, keep the peace, and facilitate family routines such as eating, relaxing, and falling asleep, according to a new national study released today by the Kaiser Family Foundation. Many parents also express satisfaction with the educational benefits of TV and how it can teach positive behaviors. The 2006 report, *The Media Family: Electronic Media in the Lives of Infants, Toddlers, Preschoolers, and Their Parents,* is based on a national survey of 1,051 parents with children age 6 months to 6 years old and a series of focus groups across the country. According to the study, in a typical day more than eight in ten (83%) children under the age of six use screen media, with those children averaging about two hours a day (1:57). Media use increases with age, from 61% of babies one year or younger who watch screen media in a typical day (for an average of 1:20) to 90% of 4 to 6 year-olds (for an average of 2:03).

In many homes, parents have created an environment where the TV is a nearly constant presence, from the living room to the dining room and the bedroom.

One in three (33%) children this age has a TV in their bedroom (19% of children ages 1 year or younger, 29% of children ages 2-3 years, and 43% of those ages 4-6 years). The most common reasons parents give for putting a TV in their child's bedroom is to free up other TVs in the house so the parent or other family members can watch their own shows (55%), to keep the child occupied so the parent can do things around the house (39%), to help the child fall asleep (30%), and as a reward for good behavior (26%). As one mother who participated in a focus group in Irvine, CA said, "Media makes life easier. We're all happier. He isn't throwing tantrums. I can get some work done."

A third (32%) of children this age live in homes where the television is on all (13%) or most (19%) of the time and a similar proportion (30%) live in homes where the TV is on during meals all (16%) or most (14%) of the time. As a focus group mother from Columbus, OH explained "The TV is on all the time. We have five TVs. At least three of those are usually on – her bedroom, the living room, and my bedroom."

Children whose parents have established these heavy TV environments spend more time watching than other children: for example, those who live in households where the TV is on all or most of the time spend an average of 25 minutes more per day watching TV (1:16 vs. 0:51), and those with a TV in their bedroom spend an average of 30 minutes more per day watching (1:19 vs. 0:49).

"Parents have a tough job, and they rely on TV in particular to help make their lives more manageable," said Vicky Rideout, vice president and director of Kaiser's Program for the Study of Entertainment Media and Health. "Parents use media to help them keep their kids occupied, calm them down, avoid family squabbles, and teach their kids the things parents are afraid they don't have time to teach themselves."

At a time when there is great debate on the merits of educational media for children, many parents are enthusiastic about its use. For example, two-thirds of parents (66%) say their child imitates positive behavior from TV, such as sharing or helping. A large majority of parents (69%) say computers mostly help children's learning, and a plurality (38%) say the same about watching TV (vs. 31% who say TV "mostly hurts" and 22% who say it doesn't have much affect either way.)

The study found that how parents feel about TV's benefits is related to how much time children spend watching. Children whose parents say TV mostly helps learning spend an average of 27 minutes more per day watching than children whose parents think TV mostly hurts. In focus groups, parents noted many specific benefits of TV viewing for their children, such as spurring imaginative play, teaching letters and words, and learning a foreign language. One mother form Irvine, CA stated, "Anything they're doing on the computer I think is learning" and another from Columbus, OH noted, "Out of the blue one day my son counted to five in Spanish. I knew immediately that he got that from Dora." Another Columbus mom said, "My daughter knows her letters from Sesame Street. I haven't had to work with her on them at all."

The following are additional key findings from the survey and attached are sample quotes from the focus groups:

Parent's Viewing Habits

• Children whose parents use screen media for more than 2 hours a day (42% of all parents) spend an average of 28 minutes more (1:14 vs. 0:46) watching TV than children whose parents watch for less than an hour (30% of all parents).

Media in the Bedroom

• Among those with TV in their bedroom, a third (33%, or 11% of all children) spend half or more of their TV-watching time watching in the bedroom.

• Among children with a TV in their bedroom, 37% (or 12% of all children) go to bed with the TV on half the time or more.

Youngest Children – Under 2 Years Old

• More than four in ten (43%) children under 2 years old watch TV every day and nearly one in five (18%) watch videos or DVDs every day.

• Most parents say they are in the same room with their child while they're watching TV either all or most of the time (88% of those whose children this age watch TV in a typical day).

• One quarter (26%) of parents with children younger than 2 years old say their child has never watched TV.

Computer Use - Digital Divide

• Eight in ten (78%) children 6 years old and under live in homes with a computer, and about seven in ten (69%) have Internet access from home. Three in ten (29%) have more than one computer.

• Among all children six and under, 43% have used a computer, and 27% use a computer several times a week or more. Among children ages four to six, 43% use a computer several times a week or more.

• There is a large gap in computer ownership, by income and parent education. For example, just over half (54%) of children in lower-income households (less than $20,000 a year) have a computer in the home compared to 95% of those from higher income homes ($75,000 a year or more).

TV and Children's Behavior

• Two-thirds (66%) of parents say they've seen their child imitate positive behaviors from TV, while 23% say they've imitated aggressive behavior, like hitting or kicking. Older boys are more likely to imitate aggressive behavior from TV (45% of 4-6 year-old boys).

• Over half (53%) of parents say that TV tends to calm their child down, while about one in six (17%) say that TV gets their child excited.

Changes in Household Media Environment and Media Use

• Since a similar survey in 2003, there have been increases in the share of children in households with at least one computer (from 73% to 78%), with Internet access (from 63% to 69%), and with high-speed Internet access (from 20% to 42%).

• There was a small but statistically significant decrease in the percent of children living in households where the television is kept on always or most of the time, from 37% in 2003 to 32% in 2005, and of children living in households where the television is on during meals always or most of the time, from 35% in 2003 to 30% in 2005.

• Among children who do each activity in a typical day, children are spending an average of 17 minutes less per day listening to music and 10 minutes less per day watching TV.[29]

A Kaiser Family Foundation study released in 2005 found that our children and teens are spending an increasing amount of time using "new media" like computers, the Internet, and video games, without cutting back on the time they spend with "old" media like TV, print, and music. The study found that young people ages 8 to 18 are using more than one medium at a time (they are multi-tasking) and that they are actually exposed an equivalent of 8 ½ hours per day although it is crammed into less than 6 ½ hours of time. The study found that the typical 8 to 18-year-old lives in a home with an average of 3.6 CD or tape players, 3.5 TVs, 3.3 radios, 2.9 VCR/DVD players, 2.1 video games consoles, and 1.5 computers. Eighty percent of young people have cable or satellite TV and fifty-five percent get premium channel packages.

The study—which measured recreational (non-school) use of TV and videos, music, video games, computers, movies, and print—found that the total amount of media content young people are exposed to each day has increased by more than an hour over the past five years (from 7:29 to 8:33), with most of the increase coming from video games (up from 0:26 to 0:49) and computers (up from 0:27 to 1:02, excluding school-work). However, because the media-use diaries indicate that the amount of time young people spend "media multi-tasking" has increased from 16% to 26% of media time, the actual number of hours devoted to media use has remained steady, at just under 6½ hours a day (going from 6:19 to 6:21), or 44½ hours a week. For example, one in four (28%) youths say they "often" (10%) or "sometimes" (18%) go online while watching TV to do something related to the show they are watching. Anywhere from a quarter to a third of kids say they are using another media "most of the time" while watching TV (24%), reading (28%), listening to music (33%), or using a computer (33%). "Kids are multi-tasking and consuming many different kinds of media all at once," said Drew Altman, Ph.D., President and CEO of the Kaiser Family Foundation. "Multi-tasking is a growing phenomenon in media use and we don't know whether it's good or bad or both."

The study also found that children's bedrooms have increasingly become multi-media centers, raising important issues about supervision and exposure to unlimited content. Two-thirds of all 8 to 18-year-olds have a TV in their room (68%), and half (49%) have a video game-player there. Increasing numbers have a VCR or DVD player (up from 36% to 54%), cable or satellite TV (from 29% to 37%), computer (from 21% to 31%), and Internet access (from 10% to 20%) in their bedroom. Those with a TV in their room spend almost 1½ hours (1:27) more in a typical day watching TV than those without a set in their room. The TV is a constant companion, outside of their bedrooms, too, in many young people's homes: Nearly two-thirds (63%) say the TV is "usually" on during meals, and half (51%) say they live in homes where the TV is left on "most" or "all" of the time, whether anyone is watching it or not.

Concerning parental rules, the study found that while prior studies indicate that parents have strong concerns about children's exposure to media, about half (53%) of all 8 to 18-year-olds say their families have no rules about TV watching. Forty-six percent say they do have rules, but just 20% say their rules are enforced "most" of the time. The study indicates that parents who impose rules and enforce them do influence the amount of time their children devote to media. Kids with TV rules that are enforced most of the time, report two hours less (2:01) daily media exposure than those from homes without rules.

"These kids are spending the equivalent of a full-time work week using media, plus overtime," said Vicky Rideout, M.A., a Kaiser Family Foundation vice president, who directed the study. "Anything that takes up that much space in their lives certainly deserves our full attention."[30]

After reading this, do you think that your children are different, and somehow immune to the bombardment of negative images, poor role models and harmful behaviors found in the E-Zone? I had a mom of two "straight A" students tell me that her kids did in fact watch a lot of TV each day (3 to 4 hours) and did all the other things "that kids these days do" in the E-Zone, but that her kids were very good students and were involved in sports as well. She was trying to convince me (and perhaps herself) that her children are not exhibiting any of the negative results found in the research and that her children seem to be immune to the harmful effects of the E-Zone. She may be correct in that her children are not yet having the problems that most of ours are (or she is in denial), but still *her children are being raised by the E-Zone*. The long-term cumulative effects of which will undoubtedly leave its imprints on impressionable children throughout all of their formative years. Whether your children currently exhibit any of the symptoms listed in the E-Zone survey or the problems found in the extensive research, you still must consider whether or not you should be trusting the E-Zone to raise your children for you.

Real Recovery: Freedom from the E-Zone's Grip

In five years you will be the same person you are now, except for three probable main influences: the people you associate with, the books you read, and the amount of interaction you have with the E-Zone. After a few years of allowing every new E-Zone device into our home, my wife and I realized that our four children were addicted to entertainment. If they were not watching TV or a movie, playing a video game, surfing the net, or listening to music, they were complaining of boredom. Any one of my children was sure to ask me at least every day (and even every couple of hours), "Dad, can we watch a movie?" We also realized that our children's behavior mirrored the behavior they'd just watched on TV or in a movie. For instance, after watching *Lilo and Stitch 2*, our kids took to the yelling they'd seen Lilo model. Not to pick on this movie alone, since even many G-rated movies and "family" TV shows exhibit behavior (mostly disrespectful or indecent) that's undesirable and unwelcome in our home. We do not allow yelling at each other, making sexual innuendos and jokes of that sort, talking back to adults, or hitting other people in our house. And yet these are the behaviors that are often modeled in even the most "family-oriented" of E-Zone shows. We don't kill people, shoot people or cut people like most video games depict, yet we seem to have no problem letting our kids enjoy this simulated violence daily. Our concern for what was happening to our kids was legitimate. The hard question we had to face was, *what do we do now?* We started with an honest self-assessment that was as basic as this:

Hours per week spent building one-on-one relationships with my children: _____

Times 52 weeks per year:_____

Hours per week children spend in the E-Zone_____

Times 52 weeks per year:_____

It wasn't hard to see that we really needed to make some positive changes without delay. So we developed a re-alistic, achievable plan to do just that, and we began to implement it with surprising success.

The 6 Steps to Recovery offered next show you what worked in our home and in the homes of other families who have taken these same steps. Hopefully your family can get back what's been lost, namely, building your home life around nourishing relationships as you interact more with each other and less with the Entertainment Zone. The word GROWTH is used as the acronym that outlines the 6 steps to recovery.

GROWTH

Gradually decrease the time spent on entertainment.

Replacement: Make a plan and follow the plan.

Observe: Know what your children are watching, playing and listening to.

Want more: Don't settle for mediocrity and a life wasted on passivity.

Throw it out: You don't need all those addictive temptations in your home.

Help: Don't try to do this alone.

SEVEN

Step #1: Incremental Weaning: Gradually decrease the time spent in the E-Zone

In the beginning, we didn't tell the kids what we were up to; we just slowly and gradually started cutting back on their entertainment. We knew we'd get a walk-out, a strike, or some other undesired response if we told them what we were planning, so we just kept it to ourselves. Some books recommend the cold turkey approach, which is "turn it all off all at once." But we thought, like a caffeine or nicotine addiction, a paced, gradual withdrawal would be easier and have greater long-term results. I have talked to families who have participated in a one-month or longer total TV turn-off and most have said that they are back to watching daily, just not as much of it. Our goal is a long-term recovery from entertainment addiction, not a short-term, temporary withdrawal.

We started by cutting back on the amount of movies we were renting and watching. We made fewer trips to the local Blockbuster, and I stopped ordering multiple movies from Netflix. We got our family down to just one movie a week, which we only watched on a non-school night. Then I cut my satellite TV subscription to the cheapest, most basic plan. There were just too many "fun to watch" shows to watch, and a lot that are complete garbage, but they come bundled together as a package. Parents are left with the arduous task of filtering out the good from the mostly bad shows. After two months, I cancelled my satellite TV subscription altogether (the kids can't watch MTV if we parents don't pay to have it piped in.) We taped the TV shows that we felt we just had to watch, and then watched them commercial-free later in the week. We did the same with events such as the Olympics.

Create an E-Zone schedule

Remember that our goal is balance in our homes. A balanced home will have limits and ideally a schedule. After the kids have finished their chores, rooms are clean, homework is finished, music lessons completed, etc., then they are allowed to use some discretionary time in the E-Zone. But the E-Zone time must come *after* the other commitments have been kept (there is often no time left before bedtime.) Stick to your bedtime schedule for your children, based on their age, and do not let the E-Zone dictate when your children go to bed. Don't let your children convince you they need three hours on the Internet to do their homework (if they are researching a paper, they may need this much time, but not typically). Each night will be different. Because of sports or music lessons, or a club activity, some nights have no E-

Zone time allotted. In our house, the TV is no longer viewed on school nights.

Record everything you want to watch on TV

You can easily cut back on the amount of TV your family watches by pre-recording everything. Most programs are at least 33% commercials. Eliminating commercials from your home will: 1) Make everyone more content with what they have, instead of wanting what they don't have; 2) Greatly reduce the amount of sexual imagery that your children see, since sex is used more than any other device to get you interested in the advertisement (shouldn't we all be embarrassed and infuriated when a perfectly good family program has a commercial break and the commercials start selling sex to our children?); 3) Allow you to stop the show for commentary, bathroom breaks, etc.; and, 4) Get everyone to bed on time, since you can now watch a long movie over two nights (how often have you all stayed up too late watching a program because you "had" to see the end of it?). 5) Come in handy for the baby-sitter—you'll know what she's showing the kids while you're out. 6) Reduce the time it takes to sit and watch an hour-long show to 40 – 45 minutes. 7) Allow you to control when you watch, rather than allowing the networks to schedule your life.

E-Zone withdrawal tips

1)   Only watch TV or movies on non-school nights.

2) Wean your family off cable. Cut back your package each month and then disconnect it.

3) Record all the shows you want to watch. Never watch "live TV" (Except for an exceptional breaking news story of considerable magnitude.)

4) Turn off all E-Zone devices for meals and whenever a guest or a member of your family arrives (this teaches your children that people are more important than the E-Zone.)

5) Limit the time spent on the Internet, playing games, text-messaging, or listening to music to 30 to 60 minutes total on school nights, and two hours total on the weekends.

6) Remove all TVs from bedrooms, kitchens and bath rooms, and get your home down to one TV. If this step is too extreme for you, at least remove the TVs from your children's rooms (or don't put them there in the first place.) Create just one room in the home that is the entertainment center for the family. This room has the large-screen TV, the DVDs, surround-sound, the video games, etc. This way the E-Zone is an open, accountable area of the home and not some thing that isolates every member of the family to their own bedrooms.

7) Do not buy all the new E-zone stuff as soon as it comes out. Your family lived without it until now, it will survive without it a little longer (and it will be cheaper in a year anyway!)

Step #2: Replacement Therapy: Finding better things to do

When my friend Kevin was attempting to quit smoking, he chewed gum instead of lighting up until the habit was broken. If your children are watching the American average of over four hours of TV per day, you'll need to plan ahead and offer them other things to replace sitting in front of the tube. Be creative and spend some time thinking about replacement ideas. Consider your children's interests and strengths. For a list of family activities, visit our website at *www.whostolethekids.com*. As with other addictive habits, the earlier you start to overcome the addiction, the better off you'll be. Children in their teens who've been addicted to the E-Zone for ten years or more will strongly resist (or rebel against) any attempts to wean them from that which has captivated their attention most of their lives. Toddlers to pre-teens will likely have a milder case of addiction and many will find that offering them replacements to the E-Zone will be much less of an ordeal. The following short lists are just some age-appropriate activities that you can pre-plan for your children:

Books. What a concept! We go to the local library at least weekly and check out books. If your children are not prone to like reading, start with really cool, really short books, so that your kids are quickly rewarded with varied stories and resolutions while their dulled tolerances to reading and listening are built up. After dinner, instead of watching TV or playing a video game, we have our children read. We sometimes read a book to them and sometimes ask them to read on their own. Exchange your weekly trip to the video rental store with a visit to the library. Your children will develop a love for reading and writing and you may be surprised—as many parents are—that some children recovered from the E-Zone actually prefer to read over watching TV after they have been out of the E-Zone for a long enough period of time.

Board games, card games and puzzles. Get the old-fashioned kind that forces you to sit together and talk to each other. Checkers, chess, Monopoly, Scrabble, Life . . . there are many more, some of which are new and exciting. Instead of buying that video game, DVD, or CD, invest that $20 in a board game that will entertain your children, but in a much more positive (and relational) way. Board and card games allow you to relate, think, strategize, laugh, and just be together. We have a table in our home that almost always has a jigsaw puzzle "in progress" on it. The kids will fill in the gaps in their free time each day, working on the puzzle either alone or together for a short while; a much better activity than slipping into the E-Zone. We enjoy card games or board games every weekend instead of watching a movie.

Musical instruments. Select a musical instrument that's right for each child to learn. If you want, learn it with them. Find a local teacher close to your home, so lessons will be easy to get to. We selected the Suzuki method of musical learning. This method allows your child to learn to play quickly by sound and learn how to read music later. Playing music will satisfy the craving that young minds have, but rather than just passively listening to music, your child will be actively creating and learning it.

Part-time jobs. When your teen-aged child works a few hours each week, he or she will have much less time for the E-Zone. If you're worried that a part-time job will hurt school performance, have your child try a one-day-a-week job on a Saturday or Sunday. You certainly don't want your child to be working so much they miss all family activities, but there is a happy balance if your child can find the right job. My friend Mike's son, Anthony, works after school three days a week for just two hours and all day Saturday. This allows Anthony to help pay for gas for the family car and have some of his own money. Anthony still has enough time each week to get all his homework done and keep up with his chores around the house (in Anthony's case, taking out the trash, keeping his room and the rec room clean, mowing the yard, and keeping the garage swept out and clean). The E-Zone will never teach our children the value of a good work ethic.

Sports and clubs. There are many excellent school and community programs for sports, music, drama, hobbies, and other leisure activities. Seek these out with your children and find ones they can enjoy. Some sports activities require a daily commitment to practice and will have a weekly game (i.e., football); others are a once-a-week practice with occasional or weekly games (i.e., karate). Parents need to guide their children to help them find an activity that the child and the family can manage, and which won't burn out either of them. We have four children and with each one of them in an activity, it can get very busy just getting each child to the right place each day. We've made a family rule that each child can take part in only one sports activity at a time. This allows the child to focus on doing their best at just one thing and helps Mom and Dad out with the costs associated with the activity and the practice and game schedules.

No family can do it all, and many try to do too much when it comes to sports programs. I've seen over and over again a family's financial and time resources consumed by a child's athletic drive. One of our friends' sons got involved in hockey. The practices, games, traveling, and financial commitments overwhelmed the family as they all tried to keep up. There were extra camps and training programs to attend, the high cost of the equipment which the son outgrew every year, the cost of personal training and the travel to games all over the state. Many sports programs have similar commitments, and each family will need to decide to what level each child can reasonably participate in. Some sports activities will have to be ruled out when you and your child "count the cost" of time and money for each activity. Beyond a certain point and level, "club" sports and even high school sports can become consuming and highly competitive. Parental wisdom is needed. Ask other parents who have been through this already with their children to see what it is you and your child are getting into.

Set limits and expectations for your children so that they aren't disappointed down the road. Another rule we live by is "If you start, you finish." We don't want our kids to learn to be quitters and to start and stop all sorts of activities. No one ever gets good at anything by having no commitment to it, and our children need to learn the discipline of sticking with things in life that become difficult. This is why it is so important to check out the sports activity in advance, talk to coaches, and parents, and really count the cost before you sign up your child and tell them to stick with it and don't quit.

Sports equipment. It's going to be hard for your children to get involved in impromptu neighborhood basketball, baseball, or other games without the proper equipment. Make sure you have balls, bats, gloves, helmets, and pads available for your children to play with. These can be expensive to buy new (especially if you have two or more children), so check the local second-hand stores or yard sales. We have a thrift store near us and we find helmets, balls, roller blades, apparel, bats, and more by looking frequently in that section of the store.

If your children are engaged in meaningful leisure activities, they won't have time to engage in the E-Zone. There are many other replacement activities that could be listed here. Be creative and talk to your children about what he or she is interested in that the family can support. Try to find a hidden or undeveloped talent that your child has and nourish it. If you're working too much to adequately participate in your child's development, consider getting a new job or having extended family or friends help out. If the cost of even used sports equipment seems too high, consider how much you can save by not buying DVDs, video games, new cell phones, or other E-Zone options. The long term benefits so exceed the temporary expenses that you're not likely to regret taking this course of action.

Step #3: Observe: Know what your children are watching, playing and listening to

I am surprised by what parents don't know about what their children are watching and listening to. We are allowing complete strangers to influence our children's minds for hours upon hours! We need to know what they are being told. Most often, we don't know the values of the internet "friend" or artist who produced or performed the entertainment our children watch. Would you willingly allow a complete stranger (famous or not) to take your children for a day and talk to them all day about their values and ideas? And yet, this *is* what we're doing by not knowing the content of the media that our children pay attention to. Why are we allowing our children to make hundreds and perhaps thousands of internet "friends?" We don't know these people or what their motives are for occupying our children's minds.

Sit down at the computer with your children and watch for one session where they go and what they do on the Internet. Next, listen to their music, watch their videos, and play their games. Do this for a week or two before you make any decisions about what to cut-out and what you allow them to continue to do. Then, talk to your child about what your observations are, and help your child think through what he's exposing his mind to.

Monitor your children's E-Zone interactions. Remember that the E-Zone is attempting to displace you as the primary influence of your children. It's not that you can't trust your children; it's that you cannot trust the E-Zone. Safeguard your family with software that tracks and limits where your children can go on the internet. Warn your children about the dangers of posting pictures or other personal information on websites. Teach them about predators, scams and key search words to stay away from. Teach them to be wise users of the internet. Don't be naive. Do not think, "My children are good kids and would not visit such a place on the internet." This passive approach to the E-Zone will severely endanger your children. It's a different world now than when we grew up and we cannot let our children be "fed to the lions" when it comes to dangers they face in the E-Zone.

Know your children's friends and what it is that your children do while they are at their friend's house. Are they watching TV, playing games, or surfing the net while away? Do their friend's parents allow the E-Zone to rule the house and raise the children?

The Litmus Test: What should you expose your mind to?

There is too much entertainment out there in the Entertainment Zone for us to take it all in. We can't see all the movies made each year, listen to all the new songs, or play all the new video games. Decisions have to be made as to what you should spend your money and time on. The mind is a precious and limited resource that we must guard and protect. We must nourish our minds and only let our minds dwell upon what is good, what is noble, what is true, what is pure, and what builds ourselves and others up. We should use the same test for viewing art and entertainment. We should admire the art that inspires us to do and think good things. The art or entertainment that hurts, slanders, maims, discredits, violates, or is in any other way destructive, should be avoided, even if it's funny or amusing. The next time you're deciding on a movie, video game or TV show for your family to watch, ask yourself these types of questions about the movie. You'll find that most movies, games, songs, TV shows, news channels, and a lot of art forms don't measure up to this standard, and are therefore not worth your valuable time. Life is short, use it well. Teach your children to be discerning about what they expose their minds to. You're their coach; coach them to focus on the positive, the noble, the good and the true.

Do not take your children to the movie theatre

What? Are you nuts? I thought this book was about balance, not prohibition! Well, not only will you save a small fortune by staying at home to watch movies, you will also spare your children's minds from the terrible previews. The worst thing about movie theatres is not the nine dollar admission, nor the five dollar popcorn, but the terrible previews that you subject your family to. I have often been embarrassed and enraged by many previews (the same goes for TV commercials.) There I am with my four small kids, expecting a nice clean, positive, uplifting "G-rated" movie. We get there early to locate good seats. Then the previews start and my children are exposed to gory killing, scary evil images, indecency, partial nudity, bad language and profane acts (and I am *paying* them to do this with my fifty dollar bill!) I've tried to cover their eyes or talk to them, but it's difficult to distract your children when you are competing with THX surround sound and a screen that is forty feet tall! This has happened to me every time I have been at the movie theatre lately and as a result I just can't bring my kids anymore (until they stop showing mature rated material to young children.) If all of us demanded better movies then the entertainment industry would produce better movies, but they are spoiled by our silence and know that many of us will go and watch anything they produce. We must set a higher standard for ourselves and for our children.

Step #4: Setting Goals: Don't settle for mediocrity and a life wasted on passivity

Ask parents if they want their children to finish high school and most will say "Of course," and look at you funny. Most of us want our children to excel in learning because we know that education will broaden their understanding and thus broaden their opportunities in life. So we want more for our children, and yet we are allowing them to be consumed by the huge E-Zone industry, which is clearly an impediment.

Part of parenting is planning ahead. We are encouraged to plan for college when our children are still in diapers. While I'm for higher education for most young adults, I believe that planning for your children's future outside the E-Zone is even more important. If you want to set your children's feet on a solid and straight path to the future, get them living outside of the E-Zone where they can learn to discover, think, create, relate and love. We've got to want more for our children and convince them to want more out of life. Where will a life in the E-Zone take them?

Step #5: Throwing it out: Reducing temptations in your home

If you were on a diet, would you keep the foods you knew you couldn't eat in your cupboards? No, you wouldn't want to tempt yourself if you were serious about losing weight. The same goes for recovering your family from E-

Zone addictions. Throw out the majority of those video/DVD titles you keep on hand. If you can't bear to throw them out, then box them all up and put the boxes somewhere out of the way. You'll find after a few months you don't need or miss them. Then try again to muster up the courage to say good-bye to them.

The Walker family had several hundred video titles stored next to the TV. The Walker children watched several movies each week. They purged their video library down to just thirty or so all-time favorites and boxed up the rest of them. They found after six months that they were no longer addicted to entertainment and sold all those old movies at a neighborhood garage sale. It can be done!

This is going to sound radical and your family might revolt, but get rid of E-Zone hardware devices in your home, including TVs, computers, video game consoles and the like. There should be no TVs in any bedrooms (yes, this includes the parents, who should lead by example). A central TV in one room of the house will allow the family to congregate to watch anything, and they'll be closer as a family, instead of isolated each in his or her corner of the house. There should only be one computer to share that has a connection to the internet. It's okay for teenagers to have a PC in their room for doing homework, but they should have to use the "family" computer to access the Web. This allows for more parental control, and also protects the children from predators, scams, and the lustful lure of dark side of the E-zone that consumes many children.

Step #6: Utilizing Help: Don't try to do it alone

Before you implement any of the following steps, it is critical that you understand the importance of both parents being united in the recovery. If one parent is committed to overcoming the addiction, but the other parent is not (perhaps an addict in denial,) then much of the progress will be undone when the kids beg for their daily portion of entertainment. If there are two parents in a home, talk through this together and make sure that you are both equally committed to the delicate intervention process. It will do the children much harm if after two weeks into this, one parent breaks down and allows the kids to go back to watching or playing whatever they want. If the parents are separated and the kids live and visit at both homes, both homes should have the same commitment to the process. One parent might get the kids halfway cured and then it's all undone with a week at the other parent's home. Put the kids first!

Caregivers, grandparents, neighbors, friends, and extended family all need to get on board, too. Our children visit the homes of family and friends now and then, and I am always disappointed when I hear they spent a good portion of their time in the E-Zone. To keep this from happening, I have had to be more proactive and talk to the responsible adult making the decisions for the children's activities and kindly ask that the kids not spend half a day lost in the E-Zone. Remember that most families use the E-Zone as a babysitter and that if your child is going to visit their house, they will likely plug your child right into the E-Zone unless you ask them not to.

Parents, you've got to get everyone on board who watches your child regularly. You know who that is. You can't do it alone. The E-Zone is too invasive, too tempting and too powerful for children to resist. We cannot allow the E-Zone to raise our children, whatever the circumstances. We have to be proactive by convincing all the caregivers and guardians of our children that we will not allow the E-Zone to raise our kids. Start by giving them this book.

One last thing about the 6-Step GROWTH recovery plan; be consistent. I have seen parents start the plan and just a few weeks into it give up. It is much better to start off slowly and stay the course. Also be very careful about being fair with children of different ages. It's easy to let your teenager slide and spend more time than he's allowed in the E-Zone that day, while making your 5 year-old stick to the plan. Keep the rules fair for all your children and for mom and dad, too. In many studies, children have reported that parental inconsistency has led them to fall back into the old habits of living life again inside the E-Zone. If you are discouraged and need help, email us or visit our website at for success stories that will encourage you. You *can* do this for your family!

EIGHT

Summary

Before the internet existed, Winston Churchill said, "A lie is half-way around the world before the truth has a chance to get it's pants on." How much more relevant that has become today, when we have companies offering 'Internet Reputation Management' and 'Identity Theft Insurance' services. The unstoppable internet is accessible from almost anywhere, yet it's less regulated than the old Wild West. And kids aren't the only ones succumbing to its powerfully addictive lures. It exposes people of all ages to a plethora of traps and dangers, including: on-line predators, internet bullying and 'e-venge,' high-powered gossip and irrepressible slander, e-mail 'phishing' and copycat websites, identity theft, web scams, shopping addictions, gambling addictions, counterfeit drugs, drug distribution without prescriptions, etc., etc. All of these pitfalls come wrapped up with the promise of providing people with an inexhaustible supply of time-consuming information and entertainment options, most of which is free for all who expand their tolerance of flashy banner ads and strategically placed links to advertisers. Our minds are being culturally trained and acclimated to consuming constant electronic stimuli, and we are exposing ourselves to more and more mental input than any other human beings in history. Fortunately for us, when our brains become exhausted from interacting with the World Wide Web, there's always the good-ol' TV waiting on stand-by to insure the constant delivery of a steady stream of visual imagery into our tired eyes!

Around the advent of television, in 1946, movie executive Darryl Zanuck predicted that TV wouldn't last six months after its introduction. He said, "People will get tired of staring at a plywood box every night." Boy, was he wrong! Today, it's hard to over-estimate the impact on our culture that stems from staring at plastic boxes every day and every night. Perhaps Bill Watterson illustrated this best in his popular comic strip 'Calvin and Hobbes,' when young Calvin is depicted as bowing down in front of his large TV, praying to it, "Oh, Great Altar of Passive Entertainment, bestow upon me Thy discordant images at such speeds as to render linear thought impossible." This elicits laughter because it's far too close to the truth for comfort!

Let's face it, we live in an age where mainstream media has been in, and is still in, a steady state of decline. Gone are the days of broadcaster's standards of excellence where media was purported to be produced in the public's best interests. The tentacles of the entertainment industry and the internet are expected to be largely self governing, and as a result, commercial interests have ruled the day. They know what kinds of media sells, and what sells is king. Entertainment today is devolving into a constant exploitation of the extremes of humanity. Pandering to our basest, most primal interests and morbid curiosities, viewers are transfixed on the most freakish of the freak shows, watching the most shocking behaviors with apparent delight. Producers lure people into public humiliation, and we watch. They offer shows depicting people eating the most grotesque things imaginable, revealing secrets that destroy families, facing temptations that tear apart marriages, gratifying shameless greed, competing to marry millionaires, endless murder mysteries both fictional and real, celebrity obsessions, tabloid journalism, talk show ambushes, gratuitous immorality, teen sex, unending violence, and let's not forget the product placements; all pushing the shock envelope further into the extremes of cultural desensitization. Producing and maintaining entertainment addictions is a highly competitive market, after all, and since ultimate success is measured in market share, demographics, and ratings, unrestrained profiteering at the expense of quality programming is justifiable, right? The Media's resulting assault on common decency has brought them great personal gain while causing great cultural loss.

News radio has become "entertainment news radio" as the emphasis is now placed on what concerts are in town, celebrity birthdays and gossip, interviews with athletes and famous celebrities, who won American Idol last night and the like. It's not popular any longer to report on local, U.S. or world news stories unless they are feeding our never ending infatuation with entertainment. Thus our general population has largely become a mob of entertainment junkies who know nothing about world events, what's going on in Washington, how policies passed by Congress impact us or where political candidates stand on issues. Our state and national political races are generally won by those who look good and talk smoothly, regardless of their voting record. Who has time to examine a candidates voting record? All we need anymore is a well produced 30-second advertisement to make up our minds on issues and candidates. No wonder we most frequently witness the sad fact that the candidate with the most money wins the race because he or she can afford more air time.

Television news broadcasts pander to commercial interests by giving us only the news that's fit to sell stuff, delivered by the most popular, and usually the most attractive, 'eye-candy journalists.' Verification of the facts can come after the fact, in fact. Most of the competing networks all synchronize their commercial slots and news topics so closely that they might as well all be one conjoined network. Most morning 'news' shows are comprised of a string of subjects that amount to elementary school drivel, appealing to the lowest common denominators. They tell us how to best pack our luggage for a trip, how to play properly with our pets, how to brighten our teeth, and they give us our fill of insultingly condescending, practically useless information. As long as it's delivered by revered Pop-Psychologists, all of our thinking has been done for us by credentialed 'experts,' at least. Instead of actually researching and reporting actual real-world news stories, many so-called 'reporters' would rather make themselves into celebrities who become the news instead of reporting the news. They are shameless in their self-promotions. These 'trusty guides' are too busy attending awards ceremonies to produce anything of real value for the people they present themselves to.

As for those we've made into rich and famous pop-idol icons in the TV, movie and music industries, they line their mantles with Oscars, Golden Globes, Emmys, Peabodys, and countless other awards, gathering together to laud and applaud one another's mutual greatness. They spend more time slapping each other on the back in congratulations for their success than they spend thinking about what effects the trash they dish out for a living will have on their adoring fans. So why *are* we their fans? Why *do* we keep watching the same old garbage?

If asked, most anyone would represent themselves by saying, "I abhor violence. I'm against the exploitation of human sexuality. I'm not at all in favor of the promotion of perversions of any kind." Yet the ratings indisputably prove beyond any doubt that people are constantly watching and thereby supporting just exactly what they would claim to be against. Why do we watch what we say we would never do? Is the effect like the train wreck that you just can't look away from? For instance, the main character in one show is a serial-killer-turned-cop who still kills, except he only kills bad guys. The show is a huge hit. People love watching this serial killer! Why? Why are so many movies and shows succeeding when the main characters are written as criminal, violent, abusive, or insane? Isn't the viewer supposed to be able to identify with the main character in a way that they can empathize with them, and vicariously experience what they experience? Aren't we supposed to care what happens to the characters as if it were happening to us? Why then, do we now seem to cheer for these bad-guy and bad-girl characters? Why is what used to be presented in a story as an antagonist now presented as a protagonist? One theory as to why this shift in storytelling has been so successful is that people secretly wish they could get away with being 'bad' themselves, but don't act it out for fear of costly consequences. So instead, they enjoy watching both fictional and real characters getting away with it.

Whatever theory accurately identifies the root causes of this phenomenon may be debatable, but it's hard to argue against the fact that what people choose to watch is a very real reflection of their own natures. Few would readily admit this, but perhaps those who enjoy watching shows that focus all of their attention on violence and murders possess some morbid interest with violence, killing, death, or dying. Perhaps the endless stream of cop and detective shows is a reflection of our fears and fascinations with the very real, very grotesque crimes that are actually occurring in the world around us. While it's no surprise that many teenagers (who are obsessed with their own emerging sexuality) want to watch as much sexually explicit material as they can get their hands on, do we stop and ask ourselves why we tend to delight in watching increasingly graphic shows about violent or perverted crimes? What's the underlying attraction? Are we really mesmerized by what we claim to hate? Or is there something darker in our nature that makes these spectacles appealing to us? I doubt many of us would be willing to consider that possibility. But at the very least, if we're honest with ourselves, we have to admit that we're far too easily drawn to, distracted by, and even sometimes addicted to things that are unhealthy and detrimental to our well-being. For our own sake, and for the sake of those we love, we need to *wake up*!

Parents and caregivers, we're both a big part of the problem *and* a big part of the solution! If we first address our own overuses and abuses of electronic media, we can lead by example and have a non-hypocritical, credible voice to impart balance to those under our care. This book is admittedly just a tiny drop of medicine in a gaping wound, but if you take its message to heart and take action on a personal level, you can make the kind of changes that will positively affect your whole household for a lifetime.

You may not be able to stem the tide of negative influences in the world, but you can fight the good fight in your own home. Use the tools at your disposal to record only limited, quality programming. Guide and monitor internet use. Consider setting aside days and even weeks without electronics throughout the year. Follow closely the guidelines and advice found in Chapter Seven. Don't let yourself be constantly occupied with useless diversions that displace your opportunities to contribute to your family. Don't let your time be wasted away on nothingness. Why rob yourself of the most satisfying of life's experiences? Why rob your family of the investment you can make with them? Will you watch your kids sign up for a lifetime apprenticeship as aspiring couch potatoes, or will you give them some real help while you still have an influence?

After speaking to a parents group one morning, a mom approached me with tears in her eyes. She explained her dilemma to me. Her son had been raised by the Entertainment Zone and was now 18 years old. As a young child he'd had all the electronic diversions that money could buy: he watched TV and movies daily in his bedroom, he had two video game systems and traded games with his friends, he had everything a child could want, but he had no quality relationships with his family. Now he's already moved out of the house and rebelled against his parents values, ideals and input into his life. He has unrealistic ideas about how money is made and just aspires to be rich and famous and make video games for a living, even though he has no idea how games are programmed or made. His mom said repeatedly to me, "he is gone, he is gone," as she cried while talking with me. I wish this were an isolated story, but I hear it all too often and try to warn parents that the years with our children pass by more quickly than we anticipate, and if we are not on guard we will accidentally allow the E-Zone to raise our families by default. We've all heard the song, "The Cats in the Cradle" where we hear a father mourn over the missed chance he had to build a relationship with his son. The commonality of this lament should remind us to take stock and re-evaluate our role in our kid's lives. I challenge you to seriously consider how many quality hours you spend with your children and compare that to the amount of time the E-Zone is influencing your children.

While living in Japan for two years as an exchange student, one year during high school and one year during college, I lived with six different host families. One thing that I was really impressed with was how much time my Japanese host parents spent teaching their children about their family history and roots. The kids knew all about their grandparents and their great-grandparents and their family tree. These kids could explain where their grandparents grew up, how they met, what they did for a living, and what they were passionate about while living. This comprehensive understanding of their rich family histories grounded the children and helped them understand what was expected of them in terms of behavior, school performance, and just being good productive people making a positive contribution to their family and to their society. My host parents really laid down a legacy for their children to follow. They essentially said, "this is who you are, this is where you've come from, and these are the sacrifices that have been made to allow you to live the life that you enjoy, so don't mess up the opportunity that's been granted to you in this life." This filial piety, as it's called, laid down a solid road map for the children in terms of a legacy they were expected to follow. Solid one-on-one relationships were built from such a planned approach by my host parents. Their disciplined communications with their kids was a part of their culture that I greatly respected and admired.

It wasn't that long ago when that kind of instruction and intimacy was more commonplace between parents and children in our own culture as well. How quickly that kind of caring communication seems to have eroded away with our fast-paced lifestyles! Kids today seem to know more about American Idol contestants than they do about American history, or even their own ancestors. Is this the kind of legacy we want to leave them with? Do we just expect our kids to automatically 'turn out good' based on genetic inheritance alone? Not everyone makes enough money to leave their kids wealthy, but is that even the primary consideration for parents? What kind of genuine inheritance will we leave to our children? What are we really passing on to the next generation if we're not giving them the best of ourselves? How can we expect to make a lasting imprint on our kids, if we passively allow any and every passing influence to consume all of their developmental consciousness? Or will we instead take action with a planned, disciplined approach to imparting our own nurturing, caring influence while we have opportunity?

Will we do what it takes to get the job done? Even if it means being unpopular with our kids for a while, will we intervene and insert balance into their distracted lives? Sure, they will complain at first. But that momentary discomfort will soon pale in comparison to the building of real tangible benefits into the lives of the people you love the most. Tolerating some whining and complaining *now* sure beats ending up with perpetually dependant, unproductive, unfulfilled adult children! We know too well that our kids don't possess the self discipline and discernment required to navigate our modern landscape on their own. It's a minefield out there today! They need our help, and they need it now, before they're sucked into electronic addictions and endless diversions that will rob them of their precious life's potential. They may not thank us for doing our due diligence now, but if we persevere in providing them with the kind of help they need, they will become the kind of people who will genuinely thank us later.

What will your legacy be?

Notes

[1]Neilson Media Research, 2000

[2]Ibid

[3]American Academy of Pediatrics: Policy Statement, Feb. 2001

[4]"Children, Violence, and the Media", A U.S. Senate Judiciary Committee Staff Report for Parents and Policy Makers, 1999.

[5]Ibid

[6]*Kids & media @ the millennium,(#1535)*, The Henry J Kaiser Family Foundation. November 1999*

[7]Ibid

[8]Plantinga, Cornelius, *Not the Way It's Supposed to Be.* Grand Rapids, MI: Wm. B. Eerdmans Publishing Co, 1995, pg. 130

[9]American Academy of Pediatrics, Vol. 104 No. 2, August, 1999

[10] University of Washington School of Medicine, Online News, Vol. 11, No. 19, May 11, 2007

[11] Zimmerman, Christakis & Meltzoff, Associations between Media Viewing and Language Development in Children Under 2 Years, 2007, The Journal of Pediatrics, Vol 151, Issue 4, Oct. 2007

[12] Reducing Children's Television-viewing time: A Qualitative Study of Parents and their Children. Pediatrics Vol. 118 No 5. November 2006, pp e1303-e1310.

[13] "Does Childhood Television Viewing Lead to Attention Problems in Asolescence? Results from a Prospective Longitudinal Study. Pediatrics Vol. 120 No. 3 September 2007, pp 532-537.

[14] China treats Internet 'addicts' Sternly", The Washington Post, Feb 22,

2007

[15]*Kids & media @ the millennium.(#1535)*, The Henry J Kaiser Family Foundation. November 1999*

[16]Huston et. al., 1992; Roberts et.al., 1999, Williams, Haertel, Haertel & Walberg, 1982; Sharif, Iman and Sargent, James D., 2006

[17]Gable & Lutz, 2000; Robinson, 1999; Dietz WH. Television, obesity and Eating Disorders. *Adolescent Medicine: State of the Art Reviews*, 1993; 4, 543-549

[18]Cynthia L. Ogden, Ph.D. et.al., Prevalence of Overweight and Obesity in the United States, 1999-2004, *JAMA*. 2006; 295:1549-1555

[19]Jean L. Wiecha, Ph.D. et.al., When Children Eat What They Watch. *Archives of Pediatrics and Adolescent Medicine*, 2006; 160:436-442

[20]Strasburger & Donnerstien, 1999; American Academy of Pediatrics, 1995

[21]Hughes, Ebata & Dollahite, 1999, Kraut et.al., 1998; Stanford Institute for quantitative Study of Society, 2000

[22]Donnerstein, Slaby, & Eron, 1994

[23]Gentile, Lynch, Linder, & Walsh, 2002

[24]Ibid

[25]*Pedriatics*, Vol. 104 No. 2, August, 1999

[26]Stasburger VC, *Adolescents and the Media. Medical and Psychological Impact*. Thousand Oaks, CA: Sage; 1995

[27]Greeson, L.E., Williams, R.A. Social Implications of Music Videos on Youth, An Analysis of the Content and Effects of MTV. *Youth & Society*, 18, 177-189; 1986

[28]*Sex on TV 4,* (#7398), The Henry J. Kaiser Family Foundation, Nov. 2005*

[29] *The Media Family: Electronic Media in the Lives of Infants, Toddlers, Preschoolers, and Their Parents(#7500),* The Henry J Kaiser Family Foundation, May 2006*

[30]*Generation M: Media in the lives of 8-18 year olds,* (#7251), The Henry J. Kaiser Family Foundation, March 2005*

*This information was reprinted with permission from the Henry J. Kaiser Family Foundation. The Kaiser Family Foundation, based in Menlo Park, California, is a nonprofit, private operating foundation focusing on the major health care issues facing the nation and is not associated with Kaiser Permanente or Kaiser Industries.

Bibliography

American Academy of Pediatrics, [webpage], URL, *www.aap.org/parents.html* (28 August 2006)

Donnerstein, E., Slaby, R.G. & Eron, L.D. The mass media and youth aggression. In Eron, L.D., Gentry, J.H., & Schlegal, P. (Editors), *Reason to hope: a psychosocial perspective on violence and youth,* 1994: 219-250. Washington D.C: American Psychological Association

Earles, K.A., Alexander, R., Johnson, M., Liverpool, J., McGhee, M. Media influences on children and adolescents; violence and sex. *Journal National Medical Association.* 2002;94:797-801

Entertainment Software Association, [webpage], *www.theesa.com* (12 May 2006)

Gable, S., & Lutz, S. Household, parent, and childhood contributions to childhood obesity. *Family Relations.* 2000; 49:293-300

Game Politics, [webpage], URL, *www.gamepolitics.com/about* (15 September 2006)

Generation M: Media in the lives of 8-18 year olds, (#7251), The Henry J. Kaiser Family Foundation, March 2005

Gentile, D.A., Lynch, P.J., Linder, J.R., & Walsh, D.A. The effects of violent video game habits on adolescent hostility, aggressive behaviors and school performance. *Journal of Adolescence,* 2004

Gerdes, Loiuise, I, Editor, *Addiction*: Opposing Viewpoints. Farmington Hills, MI: Greenhaven Press, 2005

Greeson, L.E., Williams, R.A. Social Implications of Music Videos on Youth, An Analysis of the Content and Effects of MTV. *Youth & Society,* 18, 177-189; 1986

Hughes, R., Ebata, A.T., & Dollahite, D.C. Family life in the information age. *Family Relations.* 1999; 48;5-6

Huston, A.C., Donnerstein, E., Fairchild, H., Feshbach, N.D., Katz, P.A., Murray, J.P., Rubinstein, E.A., Wilcox, B.L., & Zuckerman, D.M. (1992). *Big world, small screen: The role of television in American Society*. Lincoln, NE: Unversity of Nebraska Press.

It's child's play: Advergaming and the online marketing of food to children, (#7537), The Henry J Kaiser Family Foundation. July 2006

Kids & media @ the millennium, (#1535), The Henry J Kaiser Family Foundation. November 1999

Ogden, Cynthia L., Ph.D. et.al., Prevalence of Overweight and Obesity in the United States, 1999-2004, *JAMA*. 2006; 295:1549-1555

PBS TeacherSource, [Web Page]. URL *www.pbs.org/teachersource/media_lit/quiz_source.shtm* (26 June 2006)

Plantinga, Cornelius, *Not the way it's supposed to be*. Grand Rapids, MI: Wm. B. Eerdmans Publishing Co, 1995

Postman, Neil, *Amusing ourselves to death*. New York, NY: Penguin Books, 1985

Sex on TV 4, (# 7398), The Henry J. Kaiser Family Foundation, Nov. 2005

Sharif, I.& Sargent, J.D., (2006). Association between television, movie and video game exposure and school performance, *Pediatrics*, 2006;118:1061-1070

Stasburger, V.C., & Donnerstein, E. (1999). Children, adolescents, and the media: Issues and solutions. *Pediatrics*, 103; 129-139

The media family: Electronic media in the lives of infants, toddlers, preschoolers and their parents, (#7500), The Henry J. Kaiser Family Foundation, May 2006

If you are interested in having Gregory Bloom as a speaker please contact me directly at 303-470-8883 or visit www.honeywhostolethekids.com